This book will give you important principles to help you endure the painful decisions during times of change. Scott's insights will help your church grow stronger and reach more people for Christ. I wish I'd had this book years ago.

—Craig Groeschel, Senior Pastor, LifeChurch.tv; author, *It: How Churches and Leaders Can Get It and Keep It*

Steering through Chaos is absolutely inspirational, but it's also earthy. I love the way Scott shares simple yet profound truths that have the potential to transform your leadership.

—Mark Batterson, Lead Pastor, National Community Church; author, *Wild Goose Chase*

Scott Wilson has done it, and now he's written the manual to show us how to do it too. *Steering through Chaos* is revelational, practical, insightful, and "principle packed." Every pastor and church leader needs to read this book.

—Robert Morris, Senior Pastor, Gateway Church, Southlake, TX

I've read many books, listened to many sermons, and studied many models dealing with the topic of change and transition, and I must say that *Steering through Chaos* is one of the best. Scott Wilson captures the pain that often comes when God takes your ministry to the next level. But at the same time, he gives the reader much needed hope for the journey. Through God's grace and Scott's specific gifts, Scott has penned a manual that is profound and practical, transparent and thought-provoking, challenging and comforting. I recommend it not only for pastors but for every leader in the body of Christ.

—Eddie L. Long, Senior Pastor, New Birth Missionary Baptist Church

Steering through Chaos shows us how God's greatest promises happen only when we submit to his deepest intrusions into our lives. Scott Wilson understands that genuine change is disruptive and, ultimately, a very personal experience. His transparent communication style leaves little doubt as to why he has become such a powerful young leader.

—George Wood, Superintendent of the Assemblies of God USA

Either you will lead your personal and professional transitions, or your transitions will lead you. In either case, it is about steering through chaos. Scott Wilson personifies the principles in his book. His transparency and genius in assimilating painful transitional lessons will prevent shipwrecks for those who are in the middle of change, and he provides a map for those still in the harbor.

—Dr. Samuel R. Chand, www.samchand.com

Every growing church experiences change. Today's church leader faces the intimidating task of moving from old ministry models to new ones. Scott Wilson shares invaluable insights learned from successfully navigating the transition at the Oaks Fellowship. His book will inspire and equip you.

—John Lindell, Lead Pastor, James River Assembly

Every senior leader who is honest with himself understands that the heart of leadership is providing direction through organizational transitions. Scott Wilson understands this truth and has lived it out in his ministry. In his new book, you will have the opportunity to experience the journey and be encouraged and challenged by the principles he outlines.

—Greg Ligon, Vice President, Leadership Network

Scott Wilson hasn't written just another leadership cookbook supplying recipes that never quite seem to work as well as advertised. *Steering through Chaos* is written from his experiences with triumphs and struggles—from the real world where pastors live every day. Scott's passion to know God and his heart for lost people make his insights practical and spiritual at the same time. I recommend this book to anyone who has a vision, wants a vision, or has lost a vision. Scott Wilson has supplied us with clear guidance on how to discover and develop God's dream for our ministries.

—Earl Creps, Berkley church planter;
author, *Reverse Mentoring*

Scott Wilson represents a fresh new generation of pastors. He has successfully taken the baton from one generation of leadership and transitioned his church to the next level with gusto. This book is a must-read for the thousands of churches and leaders who desperately need to reinvent their churches to become relevant, or are fed up with the plateaus where they have settled.

—Kirk Pankratz, Senior Pastor, Church of the Harvest

Scott Wilson is a young church leader who understands and appreciates his spiritual heritage, while at the same time is keenly cognizant that the church in America is undergoing unprecedented and necessary change. Out of this natural tension, his practical experience, and his love for the church, Scott is uniquely qualified to speak to the topic of transition in a manner that is worth the attention of any church leader who is grappling with it.

—Les Welk, Superintendent, Northwest Ministry Network

It is a privilege for me to recommend *Steering through Chaos* because I know firsthand that Scott Wilson is an excellent leader. I've watched him grow one of the most dynamic churches in America. This book is filled with valuable content for anyone desiring to grow a church. Scott gives practical insight about navigating through the challenges of transition, all based on proven principles and actual experience. If you want to grow and climb to the next level in your life and ministry, this book is for you.

—Gerald Brooks, Senior Pastor, Grace Outreach Center,
Plano, TX

I love a book that takes me on a leadership journey rather than merely teaches leadership lessons. All Christian leaders—no matter their position or the size and style of their churches—should read this with their whole team. I can't wait to read it with my entire staff.

—John McKinzie, Lead Pastor, Hope Fellowship,
Frisco, TX

Scott Wilson is a great coach to me, the kind of mentor he describes in *Steering through Chaos*. His passion for Christ and his kingdom and for pastoral leadership is capsulated in this powerful book. Scott has painstakingly lived these principles, which can be applied to any ministry at any stage.

—Rick Thiemke, Lead Pastor, New Life Church,
Yorkville, IL

This book confirms what I already knew to be true: Scott Wilson is an incredible coach for pastors. I've been involved in a coaching relationship with Pastor Scott since the beginning of my tenure as lead pastor, and he has helped me navigate transition time and time again. *Steering through Chaos* takes Pastor Scott's principles and makes them available to every church leader. Add this book to your list of resources for you and your team—today.

—Jeff Kossack, Lead Pastor, Mesa First Assembly of God

If anyone can write the book on leading through transition, it's Scott Wilson. God has used Scott to lead a great church through transition and into amazing effectiveness in reaching the lost for Christ. Scott's wisdom and experience have been priceless resources to me and the church I serve. This book puts his insight into print and is a gift to pastors and leaders who want to see God do great things through their lives.

—Chad Gilligan, Lead Pastor, Calvary Assembly of God,
Toledo, OH

Scott's book has helped me understand the practical reality of leading a church through the necessary, and sometimes painful, transitions needed to become God's "unique thumbprint" in our community. His insights on leadership have made a profound impact on me and the leaders of our church. Scott's straightforward approach has helped our church take steps that we never knew how to take before. For the past year and a half, I've had the privilege of having Scott as a personal ministry consultant. I cannot imagine my ministry today without his insights. He has truly been a "dream releaser" in my life.

—Pastor Wayne Putman, Church of God of Exeter, CA

SCOTT WILSON

FOREWORD BY LEONARD SWEET

STEERING
THROUGH
CHAOS

**MAPPING A CLEAR DIRECTION FOR YOUR CHURCH
IN THE MIDST OF TRANSITION AND CHANGE**

ZONDERVAN®

ZONDERVAN.com/
AUTHORTRACKER
follow your favorite authors

ZONDERVAN

Steering through Chaos
Copyright © 2010 by Scott Wilson

This title is also available as a Zondervan ebook. Visit www.zondervan.com/ebooks.

This title is also available in a Zondervan audio edition. Visit www.zondervan.fm.

Requests for information should be addressed to:
Zondervan, *Grand Rapids, Michigan* 49530

Library of Congress Cataloging-in-Publication Data

Wilson, Scott, 1969–
    Steering through chaos : mapping a clear direction for your church in the midst
of transition and change / Scott Wilson ; foreword by Leonard Sweet.
        p. cm.
    ISBN 978-0-310-32463-8 (softcover)
        1. Church. 2. Change—Religious aspects—Christianity. I. Title.
    BV600.3.W575 2009
    254'.5—dc22   2009032591

Published in association with the literary agency of Mark Sweeney & Associates, Bonita Springs, Florida 34135

Interior design by Sherri L. Hoffman

Printed in the United States of America

10 11 12 13 14 15 · 22 21 20 19 18 17 16 15 14 13 12 11 10 9 8 7 6 5 4 3

This book is dedicated to my dad, Dr. Tom Wilson, and my mom, Brenda Wilson. I'm so proud to be their son, and I'm very grateful for their influence in my life.

My mom was the first "life coach" I ever had, and she was the primary leadership mentor in the developmental years of my life. She taught me integrity, excellence, diligence, and faithfulness. Mom would never ever let me quit.

As I entered the ministry at age seventeen, my dad became my boss, teacher, and hero. He believed in me — even when I gave him multiple reasons to doubt. His faith in me and his faithfulness to me have been the greatest factors in my leadership development as a pastor and visionary.

Dad and Mom, I'm deeply indebted to both of you. Thank you for letting me stand on your shoulders.

CONTENTS

List of Profiles   13

Foreword by Leonard Sweet   15

Acknowledgments   19

1. Turning Points and Transitions   21

As leaders, we don't avoid transitions; we create them. Our response to transitions, however, shows if we care more about God's calling or our comfort. Our ability to thrive during transitions is determined by the clarity of our vision, communication with members of our teams, authenticity, and tenacity to stay on track.

2. Vision: Where Are You Leading Us?   43

Without a crystal-clear vision, drift is inevitable and conflict unavoidable. Vision, though, doesn't appear magically. God's calling is shaped by our strengths and passions, open doors in our community, and our track record of leadership.

3. Timing Your Change for Growth   61

Every organization — including the church — experiences predictable patterns of growth and decline. Wise leaders recognize these patterns and, even more, anticipate the crucial moments when they can take advantage of momentum and propel their churches to the next level instead of sliding downward. To make bold changes when few people recognize the need for change requires leaders to be bold but also to communicate clearly and patiently with those around them.

4. Authenticity: Motivating People to Follow the Vision   77

Today, more than ever before, people want to follow leaders who have authentic faith and genuine love for them. Relational touch is no longer a luxury. Leaders have to connect with people's hearts if they want to move their hands and feet to serve God. Modeling authenticity and patience in pursuing God's vision cascades from one level of leadership to the next, instilling the whole organization with a compelling blend of warmth and passion to make a difference.

5. Corporate Prayer: Trusting God Together   101

The church may learn many lessons from the corporate world about constructing and managing systems, but we take our directions from God himself. If leaders only give lip service to trusting God, we fail to tap into our greatest resource, and we send the wrong message to our followers. During times of transition, corporate prayer transforms a leadership team and every person in the community of faith.

6. Recognizing Opportunities and Avoiding Obstacles   123

Every difficulty is an opportunity in disguise, but perception makes all the difference. Seasons and stages of a church's life provide numerous opportunities to trust God for greater things. In addition, leaders can ride waves of momentum created by new buildings, new creativity, and new strategies.

7. Celebrate Every Step of the Way   143

Many leaders are so focused on the future that they fail to notice God's incredible work in the present. Everyone, though, needs to regularly rejoice in God's goodness and in changed lives. Celebrations transform our perspective, strengthen our relationships, reinforce our vision, and give us a sense of peace.

8. The Leadership Gap: Finding a Great Coach   161

Leadership is a lonely role, and we need someone to come alongside to help us. One of the great gaps in church leadership today is that so few leaders enjoy the benefits of being coached by a competent mentor. This need isn't negotiable. We need someone who can be an accurate mirror of what's going on in our lives, stretch our vision, refresh our hearts, and help us learn to live with the ambiguity of leading people.

9. Keep the Vision Fresh   177

Many leaders become wedded to their strategy. Visions are inviolate, but strategies need to be flexible to adapt to changes, challenges, and opportunities. Keeping the vision fresh requires clear thinking and fresh infusions of heart, especially during times of transition. Continually refreshing our vision lowers our frustration level and builds confidence at every tier of the organization.

10. Endurance: Staying the Course   193

Leading people is the most rewarding role in the world, but it can also be one of the most difficult. If we aren't careful, we can get off track and fall into the ditch. The factors that threaten us are excessive burdens of responsibility and the guilt of hidden (or not-so-hidden) sins. The leader's task is to have a heart riveted on Christ, gaining hope, insight, confidence, and direction from him.

Notes   211

LIST OF PROFILES

"Changing Staff Structures"
Larry Osborne—North Coast Church: Vista, California   page 27

"Obedience to the Call"
Dino Rizzo—Healing Place Church: Baton Rouge, Louisiana   page 37

"Asking Questions"
Scott Hodge—The Orchard Aurora, Illinois   page 53

"Choosing to Change"
Dr. Sam Chand—Stockbridge, Georgia   page 67

"Communicating Change"
Tim Stevens—Granger Community Church: Granger, Indiana   page 83

"Lead *from* the Blessing"
Chris Seidman—The Branch Farmers Branch, Texas   page 115

"Risks and Rewards"
John Bishop—Living Hope Church: Vancouver, Washington   page 126

"Know Who to Listen To"
Troy Grambling—Flamingo Road Church: Cooper City, Florida   page 167

"Changing Leadership"
Randall Ross—Calvary Church: Naperville, Illinois   page 183

"Tips for Transitions"
Greg Surratt—Seacoast Church: Mount Pleasant, South Carolina   page 197

WHEN DINOSAURS ARE LED BY OSTRICHES

Wherever I go, there is an elephant in the room. It can be a youth ministry convention, a children's church seminar, a conference on preaching, or an academic lectureship on evangelism and missiology. But it's the same elephant.

You might even say that most books and articles on the church in the past twenty years are stepping around the same elephant in the room. Some books fear the elephant; other books fete the elephant. Some books cut the elephant apart to use as an ornament for their argument. Other books put the elephant in a tutu and make it perform in the circus. A few books saddle the elephant to ride over rough terrain. But the elephant always comes back to the room, dignified and discomposed at once.

The elephant is this: can the church of yesterday transition to the church of tomorrow? Or as I like to put it, can a Gutenberg-world church transition to a Google-world church? We've had five-hundred-plus years of Gutenberg practice. Google is only ten years old in October 2008.

The challenge for the church in making this transition is somewhat reflected in our differing reactions to one quote. Irish novelist John McGahern looked back on his growing up in a Gutenberg world and confessed this: "There are no days more full in childhood than those days that are not lived at all, the days lost in a book."[1] How do you feel when you read those words? Don't they sound romantic, nostalgic, even sentimental?

Now replace that last word *book* with *screen* and tell me how you react to the same quote. Can you feel the difference?

That's the elephant in the room.

The Gutenberg technology that molded our minds for the past five hundred years created a left-brained culture that emphasized logic, sequence, history, exposition, objectivity, detachment, and discipline. Change was measured and incremental.

The Google technology of our new universal medium is creating a right-brained culture that stresses immediacy, simultaneity, contingency, randomness, subjectivity, and speed.[2]

In a Google world, change is invasive and exponential. Ten years ago half of humanity had never made a phone call, and only 20 percent of humanity had regular access to communications. Today, for the first time in history, the majority of humanity is connected, both visually and, with less than ten clicks, by voice. Today, for the first time in history, one generation has watched the human population double in its lifetime; no future generation is likely to see this again. Today, for the first time in history ... I could go on and on.

By and large, official church "leaders" have taken one of two approaches to the elephant in the room. What both approaches have in common is their stick-head-in-sand, ostrich-like leadership of dinosaurs.

One approach is to admit that they and their ecclesial institutions are dinosaurs, but to bet that they can get out of the room (i.e. "retire") before the elephant fully rises. You can tell these leaders by one look into their eyes. The eyes have gone. Church has beaten the passion out of them; they are now just sockets of lies and duty.

The other approach is to deny that the elephant is there at all. The latter approach seems to be an especially human reaction. Historian David Abulafia shows how Christopher Columbus responded to the shock of the new by asserting all the time that it was not new and by trying to fit new realities into old categories (hence "Indian").[3]

Scott Wilson has written a book not to be entered into lightly, unadvisedly, or without fear and trembling. His firsthand account of what it means to transition a church from Gutenberg to Google, from a promising past to a fecund future, from safety to risk is galvanizing. His autobiographical chapter on the importance of a mentor to transitional leadership is alone worth a fortune to those trafficking in the currency of the future.

Wilson is still an ostrich, but a different kind of ostrich.

Ostriches are famous for the wrong thing: their much-mocked strategy for dealing with danger. What ostriches were most famous for among the earliest Christians was something quite different. In fact, throughout the Middle East, ostrich eggs are suspended from church ceilings as very different symbols of "ostrich-like." Often, as in the Church of the Nativity in Bethlehem, these ostrich eggs were made part of the lighting apparatus which illumined worship.

For the early church, the ostrich egg was the symbol of God's watchful care and our careful watchfulness. An ostrich egg is huge, and every predator's dream snack. So the ostrich buries its eggs deep in the desert sands and then carefully covers them over as if nothing had ever disturbed the surface. Fortunately, the eyes of the ostrich are bigger and sharper than its brains. As long as it never removes the buried eggs from its vision, it can travel miles away from its progeny without endangering their safety. But if it ever takes its eyes off the eggs, it abandons its offspring and loses its hope for the future. That is why it is said that the ostrich hatches her eggs by gazing on them, and if she suspends her gaze even for a minute or so, the eggs are addled. Or in the words of Robert Southey's poem *Thalaba the Destroyer* (1801):

> Oh! even with such a look, as fables say
> The Mother Ostrich fixes on her eggs,
> Till that intense affection
> Kindle its light of life.

The first Christians found in the symbol of the ostrich egg a reminder that they were always to "orient" themselves toward the East, toward the risen, regnant, and returning Christ, and with studied watchfulness never take their eyes off of him. That's one reason why churches were built after having been properly "oriented"—facing the East—and why to this day in Westminster

Abbey the Apostle's Creed is recited by the congregation after rising to face the East, toward the altar.

For if we lose sight of Christ, and if we abandon the Scriptures which point to Christ—Scriptures which, in the words of Saint Gregory the Great (540–604), "provide water in which lambs may gambol and elephants swim"—we will have lost our hope and forsaken our future.

Scott Wilson's approach to transition is for disciples of Jesus to recapture the meaning of Paul's words, "For me to live is Christ!" and the words of John the Baptizer, "He must increase, and I must decrease!" In the words of a poem my mother knew by heart,

> The world, I thought, belonged to me—
> goods, gold and, people, land and sea—
> where'er I walked beneath God's sky.
> In those old days, my word was "I."
> Years passed: there flashed my pathway near
> the fragment of a vision dear;
> my former word no more sufficed,
> and what I said was—"I and Christ."
> But, O, the more I looked on Him
> His glory grew, while mine grew dim;
> I shrank so small, He towered so high,
> All I dared say was—"Christ and I."
> Years more the vision held its place
> And looked me steadily in the face;
> I speak now in a humbler tone,
> And what I say is—"Christ alone."[4]

It's time dinosaurs were led by ostriches ... but the right kind of ostrich: not the one that sticks its head in the sand but the one that never takes its eyes off Christ.

— Leonard Sweet
E. Stanley Jones Professor of Evangelism,
Drew University

ACKNOWLEDGMENTS

First, I want to say thank you to the people of the Oaks. It has been a privilege and an honor to pastor you for over twenty years. You are the greatest people in the world. I love and appreciate you.

I'd also like to say a huge thank you to the church staff and board, who encouraged me and empowered me to write this book. Without their support this book wouldn't have been completed. I especially want to thank Chris Railey, Dan Call, and Jack Mourning for their contribution to the book. Thanks also to Justin Lathrop and Brian Abbott for their work and expertise in promotion and marketing.

I'd like to recognize my friend and writer Pat Springle, who helped get this book out of my heart and down on paper. Thank you for all your diligent work and guidance. You are amazing.

Finally, I would like to thank my wife, Jenni, for her encouragement and strength. I couldn't do anything without you. You are my best friend, and I love you. You and the boys—Dillon, Hunter, and Dakota—are my greatest joy. Thank you for everything.

CHAPTER 1

TURNING POINTS AND TRANSITIONS

In the church world, momentum is created by doing
something new. — ANDY STANLEY

Leaders know what it feels like to have momentum in their organizations, and they've felt the emptiness and desperation of being without it. Leaders will do almost anything to have "Big Mo," but momentum doesn't just happen. It comes only to the leaders who are willing to change personally and organizationally —those who are willing to do something new, even if that means breaking with tradition and taking significant risks.

Momentum feels like a tidal wave of energy, enthusiasm, and effectiveness—and we love it! But leaders also know that *generating* momentum comes at a high price—an increased workload and, too often, confusion and heartache. Leaders must ask themselves, What price am I willing to pay to see the kingdom of God advance and lives change?

Almost a decade ago my father was the pastor of our church, and I was transitioning from my role as the youth pastor to a new role as an associate pastor. My dad is a wonderful man and a remarkable leader. But we had a problem.

Our church wasn't growing.

Actually, that's not a completely accurate statement. The two churches my father pastored had grown to nine hundred people four different times, but each time, we hit a ceiling and fell back to six hundred. When this happened the first time, we thought it was an aberration, but by the fourth time, the lights came on, and we realized something was wrong with our paradigm.

We decided to attend Dr. John C. Maxwell's conference, Challenge 1000, to see if we could learn some principles for breaking this growth barrier and move our attendance beyond that magic number of one thousand. One of the speakers at the conference was Gerald Brooks, the senior pastor of Grace Outreach Center in Plano, Texas. As I sat in the session, Gerald suddenly said something that gripped my heart: "Your church will grow only to the level of your pain threshold." That statement would have profound implications for my future, and it would forever change the way I thought about church growth.

As I considered his words, I realized that the way we were hiring our staff, designing our programs, and training our leaders worked really well—at least until we got up to nine hundred people. But we had to face the honest truth: if we continued to follow our present methods, we'd keep hitting the same ceiling again and again. I was convinced that change was necessary, but as I sat in that conference room listening to Gerald Brooks, my vision for the future was tempered by the stunning reality that change required hard decisions that would create tremendous pain for me, my family, our staff, and the lay leaders of our church.

> My vision for the future was tempered by the stunning reality that change required hard decisions that would create tremendous pain for me, my family, our staff, and the lay leaders of our church.

When the session finished, the schedule gave us some time for a break, but I realized I had some unfinished business with God. I told the others in our group that I wanted to stay behind. As the room emptied, I found a quiet corner and poured my heart out to the Lord. I told him, "God, I'll do anything. I'll make any change you want me to make, no matter how much it costs or how much it hurts. I'll say whatever you want me to say, and I'll do what you want me to do. Lord, you love the people in our community, and many of them don't know you. Use me, God. Change me so you can use me more effectively. I don't want to just grow by having attractive services so people will come from other churches. Lord, I want to reach lost people so they are transformed by your grace. That won't happen if we keep doing the same things in the same way we've been doing them. Our church has to change—but first, Lord, you need to change me."

Something changed in me that day. I didn't come away with a profound strategy or a new program to implement. In fact, I didn't have a clue about the changes that needed to occur. I knew only one thing for sure, that I was committed to God and his process for my life. This process, I was beginning to realize, involved raising my pain threshold—my ability to deal with the chaos of change and make the difficult choices that had to be made—so that he could use me to touch more people with his love, forgiveness, and power. I thought about all the struggles and pain we had experienced just to stay on a plateau. We had worked hard to get where we were. There was pain involved in leading the church, even on the plateau. I decided that day that if I was going to suffer pain, it made more sense to endure the pain of growth, the pain that results from following a God-sized vision, rather than just enduring the pain involved in surviving each day.

CALLING VERSUS COMFORT

In my interactions with church leaders across the country, I've seen a wide range of responses to God's call.

- *I'm ready; show me the way.* Many pastors and lay leaders are passionate about honoring God in all they say and do. These leaders simply need someone to point the way for them, and they'll be off and running!
- *It's good enough.* Some leaders want their churches or ministries to grow, but they don't realize that they can't grow beyond their threshold of pain. If that's what it takes, they aren't sure they're willing to pay that price. For them, a comfortable, respectable, "nice" ministry is good enough.
- *Never again.* Other leaders have been burned before when they attempted great things for God, and they're afraid that a fresh vision, growth, and change will expose them

to too much fire again. Their hearts hear God's clear call, but their fear paralyzes them.

- *Is it always this hard?* I've also talked to a number of men and women who are in the middle of major transitions. They desperately want to please God and reach people with the gospel, but they're experiencing a host of difficulties they didn't anticipate. These brave souls need someone to come alongside and tell them, "Don't be discouraged. You're doing the right thing."

No matter which description fits you and your church, I hope this book will bring you the encouragement and strategic help you need to lead through the challenges of transition.

TRANSITIONS WE FACE

Church leaders typically experience significant transitions for two primary reasons: a vision to *expand the kingdom*, and the need *to fix problems*. In many cases, the necessity of fixing problems surfaces during a time of transition when we realize that the old systems simply can't sustain the growth we are experiencing. During these times of transition, when we begin making changes, we may find that the church continues to grow at a steady rate, experiences sporadic cycles of growth and decline, or even stops growing altogether.

When we talk about changes, we're talking about things that are directly related to the larger kingdom vision of the church. These changes can include things like adding a weekend service, changing the reporting structure of staff, building a large facility or trying to raise money for a new facility, or going from a single-site to a multisite strategy. There may be some people in the church who passionately disagree about the color of the walls in the lobby, but that's not what this book is about. We're addressing God-sized visions, kingdom purposes, and major transitions that shape the future and effectiveness of our churches.

In our fast-paced, mobile society, community demographics can change with frightening speed. One of the factors we faced a few years ago was that we had a predominantly Anglo church, but the community had become primarily African-American and Hispanic. We had to either become a multicultural church or change locations. We decided to do both. Similarly, a hundred-year-old church twenty miles north of Atlanta had served its rural community for generations, but in the blink of an eye Alpharetta became an upscale suburb of Atlanta. If the church wanted to reach the changing audience, they had to adapt their methods (but not their message). Understanding demographics isn't significant only for the U.S. Census Bureau.

> We're addressing God-sized visions, kingdom purposes, and major transitions that shape the future and effectiveness of our churches.

Church leaders need to grasp the makeup of their community, and just as important, they need to keep an eye on the cultural and demographic trends in surrounding neighborhoods. The effectiveness of the church's ministry depends on an accurate analysis of the community, and a changing community necessitates transitions in ministry and methods.

Church-growth organizations have identified ceilings that limit the growth of a church. Challenge 1000, for example, is a conference that specifically targets churches that need help breaking the one thousand barrier, as ours did. But churches face other ceilings that limit their growth. You may be facing a ceiling of one hundred, two hundred, five hundred, two thousand, or five thousand right now. Breaking through each of these ceilings requires insight, courage, and communication as you adjust your strategy and make the painful choices that will sustain growth.

In each significant transition, people and systems are stretched to be more and do more. We may face the hard reality that certain individuals, our existing staff structure, or one of the other systems that have developed over time have a limited capacity and cannot handle the added demands of growth. Changing charts and coming up with strategies isn't all that difficult. But these aren't just arbitrary names on an organizational chart; more often than not they are people who have become friends, who have laughed with us and cried with us through years of shared ministry. For many leaders, the most gut-wrenching decisions they make involve their own staff, when they realize their staff can't take the church where God wants it to go.

We may also realize that the way our staff related at one level simply doesn't work at the next level of growth. For example, as the team expands beyond six or eight people, you can't have your staff meeting in a booth at a restaurant anymore. Coordinating schedules and goals becomes more necessary—and more tedious—and the increase in communication requires more effort. When our church was fairly small, our staff meetings were simple: four or five friends getting together to talk about the things we cared about. However, when we grew to about twelve hundred attenders, I found I now had around fourteen people in my office for staff meetings. We were still good friends and we loved being together, but our ministries were plagued with mediocrity. For a long time I refused to acknowledge that we needed to change, because our staff told each other, "We have the best staff team anywhere! We really love each other. My friends in other churches are jealous of our team because our senior pastor is so close to the rest of the staff." Who doesn't want to hear comments like that? But I found that I couldn't effectively lead and supervise fourteen ministry leaders. I was wearing myself out trying to keep up with all of them, and failing miserably. I knew that something needed to change, but it wouldn't be easy.

> For many leaders, the most gut-wrenching decisions they make involve their own staff, when they realize their staff can't take the church where God wants it to go.

Inevitably, pursuing God's vision involves making changes to your staff structure, and when this happens, people on your team will face a crisis of faith. Can they trust God to transform them to be even more effective, or will they shrink back and resist the change? Unfortunately, the choice isn't always so clear. Sometimes people will agree to move into a new role for comfort's sake. They will accept the changes but will not invest themselves in the new vision and will proceed with ministry as usual. When I talked to the fourteen staff members about restructuring, at first they were agreeable to the changes. After all, we were only talking about *hypothetical* situations. But when it came time to actually change their roles and who they would report to, they realized that only four of them would be reporting directly to me. The rest would report to one of the four new executives, people who used to be their peers. Suddenly the theoretical changes became intensely personal! Even if you are a senior leader and an outstanding communicator, it's inevitable that role transitions like this will lead to misinterpretation and questions about your motives. Turf wars

CHANGING STAFF STRUCTURES
Larry Osborne
North Coast Church: Vista, California

I've faced lots of challenging leadership transitions, but none was as dicey as the transition from a casual water-cooler leadership style to a more directive executive style. It was a change I didn't want to make. I resisted as long as I could. Then one day it blew up in my face.

My preferred style is collegial. I like to hear what everyone else thinks and then make my decision. For years this pattern worked well, allowing me to build a consensus by listening to those who resisted and reframing issues in ways that they could understand and eventually buy into. As a result, most decisions felt like group decisions.

Eventually, though, the size and complexity of our staff and ministry hit a point where it was no longer possible to keep everyone in the loop. That's when the wheels came off.

The first sign that something was wrong was a radical slowdown in our speed of implementation. We had too many people in too many meetings. Every key player wanted input on every major decision. Often those who were absent when a decision was made wanted to walk through the entire process again. It drove me nuts.

The second warning sign was an increase in relational friction. A few of those who remembered the good old days balked at what they called our growing "corporateness." They missed having input on everything I decided. Some felt devalued; others were simply confused. And those who'd been around the longest liked it the least.

continued on next page…

It all blew up when the festering frustration of two longtime staff members broke out in an attempted coup. They assailed my character to the elders, claiming I had become aloof, arrogant, and unteachable. But the real issue was that I was no longer consulting *them* on major decisions. I was still being accountable, listening to others, and using a collegial style. Just with different folks.

My biggest mistake was not facing their growing frustration head-on. I knew they weren't happy. But I ignored it and hoped it would go away. I tried to patchwork as much of the old onto the new as I could. But it satisfied no one. The more I tried to go back and include anyone who felt they should be included, the more we moved at the speed of an arthritic snail. And reprocessing every decision a second time (for those who weren't there the first time) left me feeling like a Washington lobbyist — always trying to convince someone of something.

The turnaround began when I quit pretending that nothing had changed. Using an analogy I called "golf to football," I pointed out to the entire staff that size always changes patterns of relationship. The old ways had worked fine when we were smaller, but our growing complexity rendered the water-cooler approach not only obsolete but also dysfunctional.

Once the new paradigm was clearly spelled out and we had a good word picture to describe it, things quickly fell back into place. The unity, laughter, and camaraderie we once had returned. A few folks who didn't like the new normal left. But everyone else signed on, and we've since moved on to new levels of ministry and growth far beyond anything we imagined.

may develop, hurt feelings may lead to gossip, and friendships can be strained by these changes.

In addition to the challenge that transition brings to the church staff and the lay leaders, there are the added realities of stress at home. Don't underestimate the compounding effect that people's personal struggles can have during times of major transition. All change, even positive change, causes stress. In a famous study on the impact of transition, various events were assigned a numerical "life change unit" (LCU) value. To determine the weight of each event, the research team asked people of different social backgrounds to rate the degree of turmoil each event caused. Then each event was compared with getting married, which was arbitrarily given a score of fifty. The research team was surprised to find that people across the spectrum of age, sex, social position, race, culture, and education scored events very similarly.[5]

Not surprisingly, negative events and their LCU values include:

Death of a spouse   100
Divorce   73
Death of a close family member   63
Detention in jail   63
Major injury or illness   53
Being fired 47
Mortgage foreclosure   30
Trouble with boss   23

But many events commonly considered to be positive also demand significant adjustments, for instance:

Marriage   50
Marital reconciliation   45
Retirement 45
Pregnancy 40
Closing a mortgage on a new home 31
Son or daughter leaving home   29
Outstanding personal achievement 28
Start or end of education   26
Change in residence 20

These are just a few of the stresses, both positive and negative, listed in the study. Though people have different capacities for dealing with stress, when the numbers add up to fifty within six months, this number serves as a yellow warning light. These people need to pay attention to the effects of the pressure in their lives and take steps to manage their stress. And if someone experiences a total of seventy-five or more, that flashing yellow light turns red! When people endure severe levels of stress, especially for a long period of time, they risk the physical, emotional, and spiritual devastation of burnout.

Sometimes people experience multiple major stressors in a short period of time. Don't forget that the transition you are planning (or currently executing), however positive it may be, will cause stress. Take into account the reality that personal issues may compound the impact of a transition in the church. For example, in one year in our student ministry, four of our five staff experienced life-changing events. Our student pastors, Dan and Rachel Hunter, had twins after trying to get pregnant for seven years. Two other student pastors got married, and another had a baby with a severe health problem. The baby was in the hospital for six weeks, and the medical bills were astronomical. In addition to all of the chaos they were experiencing in their personal lives, their ministry grew by about two hundred and fifty students, so they had to recruit and train more adult volunteers. Except for the baby's health problems, all of these stresses were largely positive. But all of these changes, happening in such a short amount of time, produced overwhelming stress for our student ministry leaders. With their LCU values already off the chart, even the smallest changes we made in the church seemed overwhelming to them.

THRIVING THROUGH TRANSITIONS

As I write about the burden of stress we face as a part of our normal lives — and think about the added strain that transition brings — I can easily feel overwhelmed. Is change really worth it? Isn't it enough just to survive each day? I believe there are several keys that will enable leaders to do more than survive. It is possible to *thrive* in the midst of transition. To do this, though, you'll need to have a clear vision of God's calling, excellent communication, relationships of affirmation and authenticity, and tenacity.

A Clear Vision of God's Calling

The needs of lost people in our community call out to me, and we face a steep hill to climb to meet those needs more effectively. It would be a lot easier to settle for a nice, acceptable ministry, but God hasn't called us to comfort. Gerald Brooks's words continually ring in my ears: "Your church will grow only to the level of your pain threshold." Quite often I don't know what I'm supposed to do next. In fact, I don't even know what to do first! The ambiguity created by the maze of choices can paralyze me unless I reflect on the goodness and greatness of God. I may not know what to do, but I know that he does. I may not have thought through all the implications of a decision, but God knows absolutely everything, even the number of hairs on my head. My love for others may waver, but his love never fails. Ultimately, leading transitions isn't about changing the direction of the church or changing the staff. It's about God changing me as a leader so that I trust him more fully, listen to him more intently, and obey him more gladly. Jesus was completely committed to his Father's will, and his trusting obedience led him through the misunderstanding of his friends, the condemnation of his enemies, and eventually suffering and death. I remind myself that just because I'm following the Father's will doesn't mean I should expect smooth sailing, comfort, and applause. A disciple is not above his teacher. If Jesus faced challenges in ministry, I shouldn't be surprised if I do as well.

Ultimately, the vision that God gives to church leaders and pastors isn't about the size of the church, it's about God accomplishing *his* purpose, rescuing the lost and turning them into fully devoted followers of Christ. I can honestly say that the vision for our church has never been about numbers. When Christ looked at the city of Jerusalem the week before he died, he cried out because of the many people who were living in hopelessness, and his heart broke because he knew they would soon reject him. As I look out on our community, if my heart is in line with Christ's, I too will cry out when I see men and women, boys and girls in our community who are lost, distressed, and downcast, like sheep without a shepherd. Everything we do as a church is motivated by God's love for those people, and when they respond to his grace, we help them learn what it means to live for Christ with a rich, deep faith and a heart full of devotion to him. Our goal isn't to have big services or large buildings; it's to touch hearts with God's amazing love and power. The purpose of each service, meeting, class, small group, and activity is to create an opportunity in which people's lives can be eternally transformed by the power and grace of Jesus Christ.

Our goal isn't to have big services or large buildings; it's to touch hearts with God's amazing love and power.

We *expect* that God will change people's lives. Before every sermon series, we ask six questions that refocus our priorities back on God's purposes. The goal of each sermon is not mere communication of ideas; we want our messages to be about the transformation of hearts and lives. To keep ourselves on track, we ask these questions before each event:

- What is the big idea for this service?
- What do we want people to know?
- What do we want people to do?
- What do we want people to feel?
- What are the thoughts that we want people to take away from the service?
- What assignment should we give to help people apply the message?

Our goal in every worship service is to create "God moments" in which the Spirit gives insight, correction, and healing—and the strength to do God's will. After services every week, people come up and tell us how God spoke to them and changed their lives during the service. It's electric! At our church, God's vision may be as wide as the earth, but it's as personal and intimate as each individual who is touched by the Spirit in a unique way each week. Those God moments keep us going.

God may give us a kingdom-sized vision of what he wants to accomplish to touch hearts and transform families, but he seldom gives us the complete plan from the outset. In his book *Knowing God*, author and professor J. I. Packer says that we misunderstand God's wisdom if we think we are like air traffic controllers, looking at a screen to track dozens of planes going in different directions. The controllers can see everything going on in their sectors, and they can anticipate where every plane will be at any given moment. In our spiritual lives, we sometimes expect that we'll be able to see God's vision the way these air traffic controllers see the planes on their screens. Somehow we'll know exactly what God is doing in us and around us all the time. But that's not the way spiritual life works. We are, Packer says, more like drivers on a winding road in the night. Our headlights show just enough for us to make the next decision, to see whether we should turn left or right, to avoid that truck or merge between those cars. God may not give us the complete picture and every detail of the plan, but if we seek him, he'll give us enough insight to make the next choice. That's all we really need anyway.[6]

We don't manufacture God's vision for our lives and our churches in our own minds. We trust God to impart his heart and vision to us. And we don't mimic someone else's vision. We can learn a lot from others, but we need to go to God for the specific, unique vision he has for us. If we go to a conference, listen to a dynamic speaker, and try to copy the plans that others have made, we'll likely quit when things don't work out as we expect them to. If we don't spend time on our faces, waiting for God to change our hearts, we'll be tempted to take the glory for ourselves when we see God at work. The vision to lead must come from God, and the fulfillment of the vision must depend completely upon God and be for his glory. When we're convinced that we're on track with him, and his voice is so clear that we can do no other than to obey the one who has called us, then we can stand strong during tough times of transition. And those tough times will come. We can count on it. There have been times when I felt so discouraged that I had to go back to God and say, "Hey, this wasn't my idea, God! You got me into this, and I'm counting on you to give me wisdom. I'm counting on you to provide the finances. And God, you'll have to raise up leaders to accomplish what you've called us to do." And in every case, whether it was with an immediate miracle or with a longer process, God has always provided what we needed.

Excellent Communication

Many churches in transition experience resistance and conflict because they fail to communicate the vision and process in a way that invites feedback and involvement from the congregation. The key to excellent communication in times of transition isn't what's said from the pulpit; it's the patient process of informing and enlisting the support of key leaders in the church. Without them, transitions seem like a one-man promotional show, but with key leaders on board, you'll have a team of people committed to the same purpose, praying and working hard to make it a reality.

When you communicate vision to your congregation, never communicate beyond the level that your leaders have embraced. Make time to meet with key leaders, enlist their support, and then invite them to help you enlist the support of others. This process builds a wave of enthusiasm, and when the time comes to share the vision with the entire congregation, every staff member, every board member, and every volunteer leader will be nodding in hearty agreement.[7]

Relationships of Affirmation and Authenticity

I've talked to a lot of pastors and church leaders who feel tremendously lonely, and during times of transition they feel beleaguered. Spiritual leadership is a demanding role, but we don't have to face it alone. One of the most important lessons I've learned is the necessity of finding someone to coach me to be a better leader. In addition to many close friends, God has given me two men who love me enough to be honest with me, who share the wisdom they've learned, and who encourage me every step of the way. One of them is a gifted Christian counselor and senior pastor, and the other is a leadership life coach. They didn't fall out of the sky one day when I needed a wise friend. I asked God to give them to me, and he gave me wonderful, godly men to coach me and keep me on track with his call for me and our church.

In everyday life, misunderstandings easily morph into hurt feelings, which can fester into resentments. During times of transition, many people feel threatened by change, and they become increasingly defensive, fragile, and suspicious. Build unity in your team by doing two crucial things: affirm people more than ever and cultivate an environment of authenticity. When we're under stress, many of us see only what hasn't been done, and we overlook the positives around us. When the

> One of the most important lessons I've learned is the necessity of finding someone to coach me to be a better leader.

pressure is most intense, make it a point to identify and point out the good things people are doing around you. And to keep embers of hurt from bursting into full-fledged fires of resentment, ask your staff and board to be brutally honest with you about what they're thinking and feeling. After every staff meeting and board meeting, I look each person in the eyes and ask, "Is there anything we need to talk about? Are you and I okay?" I invite people to tell me about their confusion or disagreements so we can discuss them right there. Most of the time, people simply want to be sure I've heard them. They don't demand that I agree with them, but they want to be assured that I've listened to them and I understand. Sincere words of affirmation keep the wheels of relationships turning, and our commitment to authenticity propels us toward God's calling with genuine enthusiasm—and prevents a multitude of problems.

Tenacity

The magnificent stories in the Bible of men and women who followed God aren't straight-line growth patterns. Not at all. Every person used by God experienced deserts and valleys, persecution and disappointment. God called Abraham to be the father of a mighty nation, but for decades he and Sarah couldn't have children. God gave Joseph dreams that he would be a great leader, but his brothers sold him into slavery, and his master's wife tried to seduce him and then had him thrown into prison. Jeremiah was given a word from God, but it was a word of condemnation that earned him scorn from his hearers. Over and over again, following God required leaders to be incredibly courageous and tenacious, to keep going when the next step seemed hopeless.

We make detailed plans to lead a church through transitions, and we expect a flash of growth when we implement the next new thing. Sometimes that's exactly what happens, but often the moment of exponential growth comes from the accumulation of small, almost imperceptible, steps forward. Author and cultural critic Malcolm Gladwell says that organizations experience "tipping points" when something happens that propels them to the next level of effectiveness.[8] In his seminal book *Good to Great*, Jim Collins describes an organizational principle he calls "the flywheel," consisting of countless pushes that propel the wheel a little faster each time. At some point "the momentum of the thing kicks in your favor, hurling the flywheel forward, turn after turn ... whoosh! ... its own heavy weight working for you. You're pushing no harder than during the first rotation, but the flywheel goes faster and faster."[9] Gladwell would call this a tipping point. All of us would call it a breakthrough. Many leaders push on their ministry flywheel for months and years, but they give up before they experience this transformational moment. If that's where you are today, don't give up. Keep pushing, keep trusting, and look for the tipping point.

As we obey God's call and pursue the vision he gives us, we should expect some obstacles and resistance. Without a ruthlessly realistic view of the path down which God has led countless other leaders, we'll be tempted to think God has let us down. In our church, tenacity comes because we purposefully cultivate a sensitivity to God's Spirit and require that any sense of vision for the church be confirmed by all of our leaders. We're committed to listening to the Spirit's voice, communicated through the Scriptures and promptings in prayer—and not the desire to be big, the need to earn respect, or the arrogance of wanting to be in control. We want to do what God calls us to do. If the fire or the pillar of cloud moves, we want to move with it. But we can't be arrogant about hearing God's call. Though I'm the senior pastor, I never walk into a staff or board meeting and pronounce, "Thus saith the Lord! We're going to do this or that." After I've prayed, often for weeks or months, I go to our leaders and say, "This is what I sense God is saying to me about the direction he wants us to go. Will you pray and ask him to confirm that direction or lead us in a different way?" For major decisions, like the transitions we're addressing in this book, I ask for unanimity among our leaders. If God doesn't confirm his calling in each leader's heart, we keep pursuing God to ask him for clarity. It's that important. When

OBEDIENCE TO THE CALL

Dino Rizzo
Healing Place Church: Baton Rouge, Louisiana

It seems there's always *someone* who is going to fight against what you're doing for the kingdom. On the one hand, no one should expect to go into ministry with the goal of being popular. We do what we do because we have a heart for Jesus and a desire to help people. And we don't do everything perfectly. But on the other hand, criticism often comes for no good reason, and many times it comes from those within the Christian community. Criticism can be very powerful, and it takes only a few negative people to get the pastor's ear or drain the energy from the vision of an organization.

My wife, DeLynn, and I launched our church several years ago, and it was originally called Trinity Christian Center. It was a nice, safe, holy-sounding name. People could relate to it, and they kind of knew what to expect by the title. But it wasn't a very clear reflection of who we were or what God had intended us to become. Sure, we believe in the Trinity, we operate on Christian principles, and we are at least somewhat centrally located. But we also knew that God had much more in store for us than this! So a few years later when God began dealing with me about changing the name, I wasn't all that surprised. I do have to admit that I wasn't too excited about the idea of rocking the status quo.

I began asking around, checking with a few key staff to see what they thought about changing our name to the one I felt God was wanting: "Healing Place Church." Responses ranged from "Trinity is a good name, and we've earned a great reputation" and "If it ain't broke, don't fix it" to "It kinda sounds like a church that plays with snakes and sells diet pills" and "When do we start

continued on next page...

serving organic, high-fiber rice cakes?" After listening to all these reactions, I decided to put the change on hold. But God, in his own kind-but-firm way, reminded me that this wasn't something he wanted anyone's input on. This was his idea, and I had to choose between the advice of those around me and the instructions given by the God of the universe, the Creator of everything from nothing, the all-powerful, ever-loving God. When I thought about it that way, I knew what I had to do.

The next weekend at church, right before I began the message, I just did it. I stood on the stage and told everyone, "Hey, by the way, from now on we're going to be Healing Place Church, not Trinity Christian Center. Just thought you should know. Now turn in your Bibles to the book of Matthew ..." That was it. Sure, it was a little (okay, maybe a lot) abrupt, but I *knew* it was what God wanted, and the time for discussion about it was long past. And to be honest, it didn't take long for our church family to embrace it.

The moral of the story? When you obey God and follow his lead on making transitions, it will always work out the way *he* wants it to. When we are too afraid to obey or when we try to mix our ideas in the formula — that's when the plan gets messed up and the picture isn't what it should be. Ask God what to do, then obey him. While it may be scary or even uncomfortable, when all is said and done, you'll be doing the *right* thing — and that's what matters most.

God grants confirmation among the leaders, we can face any setback, hurdle, or resistance, and we'll trust God to open doors, provide finances, and grant grace so resistance is transformed into support.

During the struggles of transition, doubts and fears inevitably arise. At those moments, we need to be assured in the depths of our hearts that we haven't dreamed up this plan on our own but are following God's clear calling. With that assurance, we can face almost anything.

LOOKING AHEAD

In the rest of this book, we'll unpack many of the concepts and commitments we've briefly addressed in this chapter. Let me give you a foretaste of where we're going. In the coming chapters, we'll address the following:

- The necessity of a crystal-clear vision from God
- How to anticipate pivot points at which growth accelerates
- How to build relationships during times of transition (instead of having them destroyed by stress)
- The beauty and power of trusting God together
- How to seize opportunities and overcome obstacles
- The need to cultivate a culture of celebration
- The importance of finding a good coach to give you insight and encouragement
- How to keep the vision fresh and real
- How to endure in God's grace during times of transition

In this book, we'll look at a lot of principles and examine a host of techniques, but my main hope is that people who read it will come to the conclusion that they care far more about God's calling than their own comfort. I hope God refreshes your joy in him in such a way that you can say, "I want Christ above everything else in my life." Our desires don't mean anything if they're not directed by Christ, our love is meaningless unless it is energized by his compassion, and our hard work is idolatry if our efforts aren't for his glory. The Scriptures are full of passages that challenge my selfishness and enflame my desire to please Christ with all my heart. The Lord spoke through Jeremiah: "This is what the LORD says: 'Let not the wise man boast of his wisdom or the strong man boast of his strength or the rich man boast of his riches, but let him who boasts boast about this: that he understands and knows me, that I am the LORD, who exercises kindness, justice and righteousness on earth, for in these I delight,' declares the LORD" (Jer. 9:23–24).

I want to delight in the things that delight the heart of God. Paul wrote his purpose statement to the believers in Philippi: "I consider everything a loss compared to the surpassing greatness of knowing Christ Jesus my Lord, for whose sake I have lost all things. I consider them rubbish, that I may gain Christ" (Phil. 3:8).

And of course, Jesus' invitation and challenge grip our hearts. He told his followers, "If anyone would come after me, he must deny himself and take up his cross and follow me. For whoever wants to save his life will lose it, but whoever loses his life for me will find it" (Matt. 16:24–25).

These passages should never grow old to us. God frequently uses these Scriptures to remind me of his infinite grace, the privilege of being his child, and the challenge of living every moment of every day for him instead of for selfish gain. When leaders have wrestled their thirst for power and applause to the ground, and they're willing to say to God, "Not my will, but yours," God will use them more than they've ever dreamed. This isn't a book about growth techniques. Without a passion for Christ, strategy is only manipulation of others for selfish gain. When we long for God to be honored above ourselves, when we want God to transform individuals and restore families, when our hearts ache for lost people to know the Savior, and when we're thrilled when others are more successful than we are, we become soft clay in the Potter's hands, and he'll form us into a useful vessel. And when our hearts are right, the strategies, principles, and techniques we develop can become useful tools as we trust God's Spirit to empower us and direct us to touch lives.

> Without a passion for Christ, strategy is only manipulation of others for selfish gain.

STANDING ON THE SHOULDERS

A few years ago I had a dream. I was preaching the gospel to thousands of people in an outdoor crusade, and I was aware that God was moving in powerful ways to change countless lives. In my dream, people could only see me from my waist up because I was standing behind a huge wooden podium. But when I looked down at my feet, I realized I wasn't standing on the platform. Instead there was a big hole in the floor. My father was standing in the hole, and I was standing on his shoulders. His hands were holding my ankles, and his eyes were closed as he prayed intensely for me. At that moment I suddenly realized that all the impact I'll ever have and all the good I'll ever do for the kingdom is because I stand on my father's shoulders in ministry. He was the one who taught me, trained me, affirmed me, corrected me, and modeled a leader's life of faith day in and day out.

When I woke up that morning, I called my dad and said, "Dad, thanks for your shoulders."

A little confused, he laughed and asked, "What do you mean, son?"

I told him about the dream, and we wept together on the phone. After a few minutes I said, "Do you know what I live for, Dad? I live so that my sons can stand on my shoulders one day. And I live so that others can stand on my shoulders and serve God with their whole hearts. You gave me everything you had, and you were thrilled for me to stand on your shoulders to serve God. That's the impact I want to have on my boys and anyone else who wants to have an impact for God. That's your legacy in my life."

This image has become one of the core values of our church. We live to make people of every generation bigger, better, and stronger in their devotion to Christ and their skill in advancing his kingdom. Our goal, our delight, and our strategy is for every succeeding generation to "excel still more" in their passion and effectiveness. We don't demand that they do things the way we do them. They need to trust God for his direction and power to reach their culture. It's our pleasure and our responsibility to equip and support them.

If we care more about God's calling than our comfort, and if we care more about helping others succeed than padding our own resumes, we'll pursue God's vision with all our hearts, facing the obstacles and fears generated by change, and leading with a powerful blend of grace and strength.

At the end of each chapter, you'll find some reflection questions and exercises. I get far more out of reading books if I take a little time to wrestle with the issues. These questions are designed to help you gain insights as you begin or continue pursuing God's calling for you and your church. You can also use them to stimulate rich discussions with your staff, board of elders or deacons, and other pastors. Don't rush through these questions. Ask God to use them to stimulate your faith, sharpen your vision, and shape your strategy.

MAPPING YOUR DIRECTION

1. What do you think it means to "care more about God's calling than our comfort"? Who do you know who exemplifies this conviction? What are the costs involved? Is this attitude attractive to you? Why or why not?

2. On a scale of zero to ten, what is your pain threshold, the most you are willing to suffer for Christ and his kingdom? How can you tell what it is? Are you satisfied with it? Why or why not?

3. What major ministry transitions have you experienced in the past five years? What transition do you face today?

4. Describe the way personal stresses compound the pressures experienced in transitions. Give some examples from your own experience.

5. Give yourself (and your team) a reality check to determine how you are positioned to thrive in transition. Evaluate your proficiency in the following:

   - A clear vision of God's calling
   - Excellent communication
   - Relationships of affirmation and authenticity
   - Tenacity

6. What do you hope God will do in your life as you read this book? What are your specific goals for reading it and applying the principles?

CHAPTER 2

VISION

Where Are You Leading Us?

*God calls us to himself so decisively that everything we are,
everything we do, and everything we have is invested with
a special devotion and dynamism lived out as a response
to his summons and service.* — OS GUINNESS

A few years ago a pastor called and asked me to meet with him. He needed help bringing a fresh vision to his church and equipping his people to reach out to the local community. The church had been in existence for about forty years, but the pastor was fairly new to the church and had only recently become the senior pastor. I met with him for several hours and asked him a series of questions to get a sense of his vision for the church. At one point I asked him to show me the stated purpose of the church — their mission statement. He pulled out a piece of paper. On it was written, "Connecting with God and Each Other." This had been the vision statement for the church for several years, and it was on all of their literature — their bulletins, brochures, and newsletters.

I asked the pastor to schedule appointments for me to talk to the top thirty church leaders so I could take their corporate temperature. Meeting with them in small groups over a period of several hours, I asked them one primary question: "When people ask, 'What is this church all about?' what do you tell them?" Surprisingly, only one of the thirty leaders came close to the written statement. The rest of them said things like, "We should be the friendliest church in town," "We don't just sit in the pews;

we serve," "We're committed to reaching the lost all around the world," and on and on.

Now, none of these are bad things. In fact, they are all worthy goals for ministry. But these thirty people—the leaders of the church—couldn't even articulate the single, most compelling heartbeat of the church. In fact, in my conversations with them, something very strange happened. Very quickly they turned from stating what they *thought* the mission statement actually said to lobbying for what it *ought* to be! Many of them said things like, "Well, *I* think we should be putting a lot more into youth ministry" or women's ministry or missions or service in the community or prayer or Bible study or any of a dozen other worthwhile things. Again, these things weren't wrong, but the church leaders weren't speaking with one heart and one voice with a common language. (I didn't have to ask what role each of them played in the church. Each one advocated a purpose that focused on his or her area of ministry: prayer, children, missions, adult education, and so on.) When I reported these conversations to the pastor, the lights suddenly went on for him. He began to realize why he was having so much trouble aligning people with the church's vision: they didn't even know what it was!

Staff and lay leaders aren't the only ones who sometimes get foggy about the vision for a church. A consultant who helps churches with fundraising campaigns told me that when he meets with pastors, he regularly asks them about their church's vision statement. He told me that many of these pastors can't even articulate the purpose for their church, and yet they want to talk with him about enlisting their people to spend millions of dollars on a building project!

THUMBPRINT

When I want to fly from Dallas to San Diego, I don't just pick a plane and wait for the pilot to ask, "Where do all of you want to go today? Take a vote and let me know." That would be crazy! But if you think about it, that's how a lot of churches treat their sense of destiny—they put it up for a vote. Personally,

I don't think that's the way God intends for pastors to shepherd his people.

In one sense, the purpose and vision of every local congregation on the planet, from Pentecost until today, is exactly the same: to fulfill the Great Commandment and the Great Commission. This global, universal vision statement won't change until the Lord returns, but every local body of believers has its own unique way of living out this God-sized vision. Most often this precise calling is found at the intersection of the pastor's spiritual gifts and passions, the demographics of the area, and the needs of the people in that community. When God calls a pastor to lead a church, it's a holy calling. God gives each leader a set of talents, natural abilities, and spiritual gifts that they can use to advance the kingdom, and the church's culture and style frequently become a reflection of these talents. If a pastor is a gifted evangelist, the ministry of the church will often focus primarily, but never exclusively, on reaching the lost. If a pastor is an outstanding Bible teacher, people will flock to hear God's Word applied to their hearts. If a pastor is an excellent leader, he will enlist and train scores, hundreds, or even thousands to become leaders in God's army. Our church is known for reaching lost people, teaching the Scriptures, and multiplying leaders. These, not surprisingly, are the gifts God has given me to use for his glory, and I use them as effectively as I can.

> Every local body of believers has its own unique way of living out this God-sized vision.

This perspective takes on ultimate importance when a church wants to hire a pastor. Does the vision of the church shape the leader, or does the leader shape the vision of the church? The answer is yes! Both are true. Churches who interview a prospective senior pastor need to understand that the leader's gifts and passions will, to a large extent, shape the vision and direction of the church for years to come. If they are looking for a change in direction, they need to hire someone who already embodies that change and has demonstrated excellence in the new strategy and direction, not someone who says he hopes he can make it happen someday. I know a pastor who was interviewed by a church board. He was very clear about his qualifications and experience. They believed God wanted to bring significant change to their church, and they said he was exactly the kind of leader they were looking for. The board unanimously invited him to be their pastor. Two months later four of the nine board members left the church, but out of conviction, not anger. They were able to honestly say, "I know he's the right man, and I'm convinced the direction is right, but I don't feel qualified to help the transition take place." These were men of the highest integrity who grasped God's vision for the future and were honest enough to know they weren't capable of helping it occur. At the moment the new pastor was hired, his thumbprint was already on the church, and these board members were willing to pay a significant price to make his vision a reality.

Some pastors, though, have a cloudy sense of vision that they've borrowed from someone else. While learning from others is essential, each leader must do the hard work of pursuing God for their own vision. Before Jesus began his earthly ministry, the Spirit led him into the desert for forty days. There he was tempted by Satan, and when he emerged, he began the most remarkable ministry history will ever know. Throughout church history, men and women who have been used mightily by God began by passionately pursuing God. God-given vision won't come from a seminar, a seminary, or a nationally known leader. It is a gift from God.

> They live for the *urgent and screaming* instead of the *important but often hidden.*

For some pastors, staff, and lay leaders, the pace of life is so hectic that they fail to carve out enough time to reflect very deeply about the things that really matter in ministry. They live for the *urgent and screaming* instead of the *important but often hidden.* In his article "Diagnosing Hurry Sickness" in *Leadership* magazine, John Ortberg identifies two signs of pace-related stress in church leaders — speeding up and multitasking:

1. "*Speeding up.* You are haunted by the fear that you don't have enough time to do what needs to be done. You try

to read faster, lead board meetings more efficiently, write sermons on the fly, and when counseling, you nod more often to encourage the counselee to accelerate."

2. *"Multi-tasking.* You find yourself doing or thinking more than one thing at a time. The car is a favorite place for this. Hurry-sick pastors may drive, eat, drink coffee, listen to tapes for sermon ideas, shave or apply make-up, direct church business on the car phone—all at the same time. Or they may try to watch TV, read *Leadership*, eat dinner, and carry on a phone conversation simultaneously."[10]

Thousands of pastors have cloudy visions because they are on the verge of burnout. They have poured their lives out for others for years, and they didn't find the sense of rest and balance they needed in order to keep going. When they felt lonely, they just worked harder to fill the emptiness. When they felt used or accused, they pushed themselves even harder to earn approval. When they felt trapped by meaningless work, they tried to find diversions to entertain themselves. Burnout is one of the most common and dangerous conditions for those in ministry. People who are stressed to the breaking point will lack creativity and passion. They won't have the resilience needed to face resistance. They simply must find a friend, a mentor, or a counselor to give them perspective and hope.

In a similar way, the needs that we encounter in every community are the same ones we find all over the world. People all over the world stand in need of Christ's forgiveness; there are families that need to be reconciled, parents who need to model grace and strength to their children, and people who need to learn to handle their resources wisely. But we also need to dig a little deeper, to discover the specific opportunities and unique obstacles that define the character of our community. For example, a suburban church near Houston took a long, hard look at their community, and they realized that an unusually large segment of the people living nearby were young parents. They also noticed that the affluence of the community provided a destructive blend of disposable income and boredom—an explosive mixture! Alcohol and drugs were devastating individual lives and destroying families. The pastor and his leadership team asked God for clear direction, and God led them to prioritize three ministries for the next decade: parenting, recovery, and serving "the least of these." While the first two ministries may seem like no-brainers, the leaders also recognized that if people weren't being encouraged to use their wealth for Christ's kingdom, serving those in need, they'd be tempted to waste it on frivolous, meaningless things. These three ministries formed the heart of the church's vision, and every activity the church pursues, from evangelism to children's ministry, is now targeted to meet needs in each of these three areas.

As we asked God to clarify our vision at the Oaks Fellowship, I asked our staff and board three questions:

1. What do we do exceptionally well?
2. What are we passionate about?
3. What are the demographics of our community?

First, we discussed the things that we do well. In other words, how has God already put his thumbprint on our life as a church? We had some wonderful, rich discussions, and one of the things that surfaced was that we're really good at building leaders. In the past few years more than two hundred young people from our church have gone into some type of full-time ministry. That seems to be a pretty strong thumbprint that we need to continue nurturing and developing. When we studied the demographics of our community, we also found that 85 percent of the families in our area have children who live at home. We recognized this as an open door, and we intentionally tailored all of our activities to involve parents and children. We wanted people in our community to say, "That church really cares about the things I care about, and they give me exactly what I need to be the best parent I can be. They also provide outstanding resources for my children. I can't imagine a better place to worship or a better partnership to help me raise my children to follow Christ." Our programming for parents and children comes at the intersection of parental need, a shared passion to love kids, and the skills of our trained leaders. We want to help every father, mother, and grandparent be the best parent or caregiver that they can be, and we are committed to equipping the next generation to be bigger, better, and stronger in their love for Christ. For us, "equipping the next generation" isn't just a phrase we have on a paper filed away in a desk drawer. It's a vision and strategy that has become ingrained in our souls, and we live out this vision every day.

Most of us can benefit by *expanding* our vision statement by adding a succinct set of value propositions. These values put flesh on the vision's bones and describe the specific elements of what the vision looks like in day-to-day operations. At our church, we have four values that reflect who we are and what we believe God wants us to be and do. Like our vision statement, our values never change. Our strategies change, but our vision and values remain constant over time.

Our church's vision is, "Helping people become fully devoted followers of Christ." In our new phase of transition and growth, our theme is, "Experience the Impossible." We want people to realize that God can do absolutely anything. From time to time we may feel hopeless, but we serve a mighty God who can accomplish things we never dreamed possible. As we are gripped with his greatness and love, we'll believe him for more. Our church's values, stated and explained, are written for everyone to read and for leaders to absorb:

- *It's about leading leaders.* The world is sick and must get better. Have you looked around lately? Check out the nightly news for five minutes and you'll agree. So what are we supposed to do? Sit back and watch it crash? Whether you're an award-winning corporate bigwig or take care of your kids at home every day, you can make a difference that matters. You can resist the temptation to go with the flow and unleash the leader within you—and see the world change now.

- *It's about "multi-sight" strategy.* We believe in the concept of focused vision. Who doesn't? But when an exciting opportunity comes along, we want to be flexible enough to respond. Our goal is to get solid leadership in place and then be ready for something new. Our multisite strategy personifies this. We aren't satisfied to keep our eye on three or four locations; there are far too many hurting communities out there. We intentionally have our eye on several locations, but with one goal in mind: seeing God change communities.

- *It's about creating the future.* We need to learn from the mistakes of the past. And we need to make the most of today, seizing the opportunities that God provides. But we can't stop thinking about tomorrow as well. What we did yesterday and what we do today ... creates tomorrow. When we are intentional about the choices we make each day, we are able to create a better future for our communities, our families, and ourselves. Where will you be in twenty years? What will your church look like? Answering these questions begins today.

- *It's about moments that change you forever.* Your first kiss. Your wedding day. The birth of a child. When you gave your heart to God. A sacred connection with God during worship. Moments like these are unforgettable ... and they change you forever. We hunger for holy moments when we can connect with God. It's a hunger that can't be satisfied. Together we'll pursue these moments with God and allow him to mold us into the people we need to be. We're always looking for one more moment, just one more that will change us forever.

Every leader in our church can repeat this vision and these value statements, which form the template for all of our planning.

If something sounds like a great thing to do but doesn't fit our vision and values, we don't do it. It's that simple.

The value of "moments that change you forever" is especially poignant to me. From the outset of the church, we didn't just want to have good services; we wanted to create moments in which almighty God changed lives—nothing less than that. We began to pray, and as we watched God work, we began to expect this kind of response in every single event we hosted. Now after each service, I stand at the door to meet the new people who have come to the church. As I meet them, I hear about the incredible, life-changing moments that are happening in people's lives, and they thrill my heart. Recently a lady came up to me with her husband by her side. She said, "Do you want to see a miracle?"

> If something sounds like a great thing to do but doesn't fit our vision and values, we don't do it.

I smiled and said, "Sure I do."

She didn't say a word. She just stood there with her husband and grinned. I felt kind of dense because I didn't understand. I asked, "Okay, where's the miracle?"

"You're looking at it," she told me. "A year ago I hated my husband and he hated me. Our situation was impossible, but God worked in our lives, and now we love each other more than ever before. It's a miracle!"

People tell me about God's Spirit changing hearts so that broken relationships are restored, addicts find Christ and sobriety, prisoners come to faith and are invited into the family of God and experience hope for the first time in their lives, and rage is transformed into love, and they tell me about countless other "God moments" that began or continued in our services. The expectation that God is going to work sharpens our preparation and infuses us with passion, and we are thrilled when God meets our expectation each week. To me, it just doesn't get any better than that!

Young leaders often feel frustrated because their vision isn't as clear as they'd like it to be. They long to be consumed by a purpose that captures their whole hearts and demands every fiber of their being. I was one of them. When I was nineteen, I went to a conference to hear Pastor Tommy Barnett preach. He is the senior pastor of Phoenix First Assembly in Arizona, and he has always been a great hero to me. In his inimitable style, he challenged us, "Find a need and fill it. Find a hurt and heal it." As the session ended, I cried out to God in frustration, "God, why don't I have a calling like that? Why don't I have a burning passion like Tommy Barnett has? If you'd give me a vision like that, I'd do it, but God, you haven't told me yet!"

A little while later I had lunch with my dad. He took one look at me and asked, "Son, what's wrong?"

I told him about my frustration, and as always he gave me great advice. He said, "Scott, be faithful in the little things, and someday God will give you a vision that's bigger than you could ever dream of or ask for. For now, just love God and love people, and don't worry about what your ultimate purpose will be. God will make it clear when the time is right. You can count on it." That's God's wisdom for all of us, and especially for young people (or new believers) who long for a clear, compelling, definitive sense of purpose for their lives.

Vision isn't something I *determine*—it's something I *discover* as I walk with God day after day. And it doesn't come in a neat package all at once. We shouldn't copy anyone else's vision, but we can learn a lot from countless leaders who have wrestled with God about their calling. I am a voracious reader, and I've listened to gifted leaders talk about their pursuit of God. I've gained insight from Bill Hybels, Andy Stanley, Craig Groeschel, and many others. None of them gave me their vision in its entirety, but statements, strategies, and stories from each of them resonated in my heart. These became the building blocks God used to construct my calling and help me discover my gifts, my passion, and the needs of those around me. As I listened to each of them, I had to do the work of winnowing the wheat from the chaff, sorting out what fit me and my situation and what didn't. I've had many, many conversations with friends and mentors who add value to my vision and calling.

> Vision isn't something I *determine*—it's something I *discover* as I walk with God day after day.

ASKING QUESTIONS
Scott Hodge
The Orchard: Aurora, Illinois

Isn't it funny how when we're kids, we ask lots and lots of questions, but as we get older, we tend to ask fewer and fewer?

Why is that?

Is it because questions force us to get honest with ourselves? Or because they seem to rip apart the assumptions that we tend to buy into? Those same assumptions that so often end up guiding our movements? Maybe we just don't like the answers we are likely to receive.

As difficult and challenging as asking questions can be, when a church or organization is facing a crisis or a need for change, asking the tough questions that no one wants to ask can be one of the healthiest and most freeing steps we can take. During our journey of transition at The Orchard, we found ourselves asking a ton of questions. Questions like:

Who has God best positioned us to reach?

What are we currently doing that is making it difficult to reach people?

What do we need to stop doing?

What do we need to start doing?

Is this event or ministry helping or hindering our efforts to reach people?

Those were some pretty eye-opening questions! But guess what? Throughout the process of answering them, we discovered the specific steps and actions needed to turn our dying, eighty-year-old church in a new direction.

There is freedom in the truth. Jesus said it this way: "You will know the truth, and the truth will set you free" (John 8:32). Is your church or organization stuck in a rut? Are you looking for the freedom to move ahead with fresh ideas and vision? Start by asking questions! It may be a painful process in the short term, but eventually the answers you get will open your eyes to the truth. And once you know the truth, your church will be free to follow God.

For a few leaders, God suddenly gives them a clear, compelling vision into which they'll pour their hearts for the rest of their lives. As a young man, William Wilberforce served in Britain's House of Parliament. After he became a Christian, he reflected on God's intention for his life, and soon he was convinced of his purpose. He wrote perhaps the shortest and most challenging vision statement I've ever read: "God Almighty has set before me two great objects, the suppression of the Slave Trade and the Reformation of Manners [turning people from vice to virtue]." England was the world's greatest sea power, and much of its commerce was based on slave labor. For this reason, powerful forces in government and industry opposed Wilberforce's efforts to free the slaves. On several occasions he was physically beaten, and often he was verbally ridiculed, but he was resolute in his purpose. Just days before he died, news reached him that a bill had passed to outlaw the slave trade. His vision was fulfilled.

For the vast majority of us, however, God takes a different tack. As we pursue him, he gradually uncovers more of the picture of our purpose while we take steps to obey what he has already shown us. It's like seeing a billboard way down the highway. As we get closer, it becomes clearer. The shapes that were undefined earlier make sense, we can read the words on the ad, and we notice the relationship between elements of the message. None of that was obvious when we were farther back. We had to get closer to grasp the real meaning. In the same way, we shouldn't be frustrated if we find that we misunderstood some of the specifics of God's calling. It's part of the process to pursue, to try and fail, and to try and see God work in incredible ways. As the pattern of God's blessing becomes clear, we sense his pleasure and his power, and we gain confidence that we're on track with him. But no matter how old we get, we still need to grow closer to God and keep learning to follow him more closely. In fact, as we age, God may change our job description so he can use our experiences—the bad as well as the good—to teach and train others.

F.O.C.U.S.

One of the most important aspects of my calling as a pastor is the realization that I'm not gifted and equipped to do certain things. Every leader needs to have a "don't do" list as well as a "to do" list. If not, we'll be overwhelmed. Every church has endless opportunities to serve, and every community has endless needs to be met. If I stretch myself too thin, I won't be very good at anything, and I'll neglect to devote enough energy and passion into the things God has actually called me to do.

When I became a senior pastor, I tried to do way too much. I wanted to serve, and I wanted to pour out my life for God, but I didn't understand the importance of setting priorities. Early one morning I sat bolt upright in my bed at exactly five o'clock, and out of my mouth came the word *focus*. I said, "Lord, I don't know what this is about, but I think you're trying to tell me something."

> If I stretch myself too thin, I won't be very good at anything, and I'll neglect to devote enough energy and passion into the things God has actually called me to do.

I got up and found a quiet place so I didn't wake anybody, and I listened to God. He impressed me with this thought: "There are things on your calendar that I didn't put there."

I was incensed. "What do you mean? Everything on my calendar is for you — everything!"

Gently God told me, "Yes, you're doing all that *for* me, but I didn't *call* you to do many of those things. There's a difference. You're doing too much. That's why you're stressed out and so full of anxiety."

"Okay, Lord," I answered, "what do you want me to do?"

"I want you to focus," he told me. "I've given you strength, passion, and anointing to do the things I've called you to do, but every time you say yes to something else, you're effectively saying no to me. You have to focus and cut out everything I haven't called you to do. I've called other people to do those things. Don't rob me of your best, and don't rob them of their privilege to serve me."

Instantly an acrostic came to mind, and I wrote it down:

F — First things first.
O — Other things second.
C — Cut out the unimportant.
U — Unify behind vision.
S — Stick with it.

A little while later Jenni woke up, and I told her about my encounter with God. I told her, "I've got to focus."

She looked at me the way wise wives do, and she said, "I'm glad God told you that. It's what I've been trying to tell you for months. Maybe you'll listen to him."

Some of us have a "savior complex," and we think it's our job to fix every person's problem and meet every need. When we succeed, we feel indispensable, but when we fail, we feel ashamed. We run from need to need and person to person, but we only drive ourselves and our families crazy. We need to remember that the Savior's job is already taken. Our role is a bit more limited than his.

> We aren't the only church or ministry in town, and we don't have to be all things to all people.

As a church, we don't need to recreate the wheel to meet every need. We aren't the only church or ministry in town, and we don't have to be all things to all people. We must minister within the context of our God-given vision and focus. But that doesn't mean we can't partner with some wonderful local, national, and international organizations, from a local food pantry to overseas missions, to share our resources and gain the benefit of their infrastructure and experience.

CALLING AND CONCEIT

Grand visions—and any measure of success in fulfilling those visions—inevitably carry with them a dark side: the temptation to take credit for all the blessings. For many people, it's easier to trust God through difficulties than to humbly trust him in times of harvest. It's sad, but it's human nature. As we stretch ourselves to seek God with all our hearts and ask him to use us to advance his kingdom, we need to be very much aware of the dark side of our hearts: our thirst for personal glory.

God's calling encompasses all we are, all we have, and all we do. As Paul wrote to the believers in Rome, "From him and through him and to him are all things. To him be the glory forever! Amen" (Rom. 11:36). God's purpose for us reached us when we were at our worst, and by his great grace transformed us into useful and usable tools in his hands. In the same letter (Rom. 5:1–11), Paul describes those apart from Christ as "sinners" (v. 8) who are "powerless" (v. 6) "enemies of God" (v. 10). Not a pretty picture! To the Ephesians, Paul says we were "dead" in our sins, but God "made us alive" in him (Eph. 2:1–9). We who were far away from God and without any semblance of hope were chosen, adopted, forgiven, and sealed by the Holy Spirit (Eph. 1:1–14). Now God has given us, as his children, the unspeakable privilege of representing him as his ambassadors to take the word of reconciliation to every person on the planet. We deserved eternal condemnation, but we've received his matchless love, grace, power, and a role higher and more prestigious than anyone could ever imagine! Some people say we need to go beyond the gospel into "deeper truth," but the message of the gospel encompasses the full range of truths about God rescuing us from sin and death, his sacrifice, his infinite love, our adoption into his family, and the privilege of serving him all day, every day. Personally, I don't think I'll ever get over the bedrock truth and grace of the gospel of Christ, nor should I.

But we are forgetful people. We can get so caught up with the things that cry out for immediate attention that we fail to remember the overwhelming truth of God's grace. And when we forget his grace, we can easily fall prey to one (or both) of the twin errors of false humility and selfish conceit. Paul advised the Roman Christians, "By the grace given me I say to every one of you: Do not think of yourself more highly than you ought, but rather think of yourself with sober judgment, in accordance with the measure of faith God has given you" (Rom. 12:3). "Sober judgment" means that we remember who we are, where we've come from, and who it is that we serve. False humility says, "I'm scum. I can't do anything. If God does anything good, it's in spite of me." That kind of statement may sound very humble, but it denies that God created us to do great works for him and that we are children of the King, ambassadors with a high calling. Some of us fall off the other side of the table: we see God use us, and soon we believe we're indispensable to God. "Isn't he lucky to have me on his side?" we think. Some of us flip-flop between the two extremes. They are actually two sides of the same coin—the desire to get approval and worth by winning the applause of others.

The truth is that every ability we have, every talent we possess, every spiritual gift we use, and every attractive personality trait we demonstrate is a gift from God to be used with gratitude and passion. When we remember the awesome grace of God and his gifts to us, we are genuinely thankful, not falsely humble, and all of our efforts are designed for one purpose: to please the one who bought us, rescued us, and loves us so much. We live for an "audience of one," not the applause of many.

As we lead our churches to touch more people, genuine humility and gratitude keep us grounded. We aren't as defensive when people disagree, and we aren't as impatient when people are slow to get on board. We love more, and we laugh more. We use our abilities with skill and power, and we thank God every day for the privilege of being used by him. When we aren't driven to prove ourselves or please others to win their approval, we can breathe a bit more easily and make it a priority to spend quality time with God and with our families. As our trust level goes up, our stress level goes down. Too many of us equate stress with passion. We think that if we really care about God and his cause, our lives will necessarily be intense all day, every day. That's not true at all. If we really care about Christ and what he's called us to do, we'll take care of our hearts, our families, and our bodies. We'll make sure we spend time with friends and mentors to give us perspective and keep us from getting off track, and we'll trust God to guide us in his direction, in his ways, and in his timing. Our lives will be characterized by a beautiful blend of contentment and passion, and countless people around us will benefit from following our example.

> If we really care about Christ and what he's called us to do, we'll take care of our hearts, our families, and our bodies.

MAPPING YOUR DIRECTION

1. On a scale of zero to ten, how clear and compelling is your sense of vision today? Explain your answer.

2. Reflect about and write your answers to these three questions:

   - What am I (what is our church) good at? (What are we known for? What do we have confidence in doing? What do we do that others see as a model for them to learn from?)
   - What are we passionate about? (What do we love to talk about? What makes us laugh and cry? What are our dreams?)
   - What are the demographics of our community? (What are the trends of the past few years? Where is the community heading? What are the open doors for ministry? What are the obstacles?)

3. What things distract you from your calling and from fulfilling God's vision?

4. What are some specific steps you need to take to focus on the most important things?

5. Describe false humility and selfish conceit. Then describe the powerful blend of contentment and passion that comes from seeing every ability and opportunity to serve as a gift from God.

6. Based on what you've learned in this chapter and your reflection on these questions, write a plan for clarifying your vision and values so they become compelling to you, your team, and your church. How will you know when your vision is truly clear and compelling?

CHAPTER 3

TIMING YOUR CHANGE FOR GROWTH

It is in the crucible of chaos that God forms our character and
determines our destiny. — DR. SAMUEL R. CHAND

Several years ago, before we had multiple locations, our church
in Oak Cliff was doing really well. Our debt was paid off,
people were coming to Christ, and great things were happening.
My father (who was senior pastor at the time) told the church,
"We need to ask God what his plans are for our church." We were
open to whatever God wanted us to do, but none of us had ever
imagined that God would want us to start a church in a different location. In our denomination, the church in Oak Cliff was
sacred ground. Historic revivals had been held there. People like
Oral Roberts, Jack Coe, Gordon Lindsay, and many of the Voice
of Healing ministers had strong ties to our local assembly back in
the day. The who's who of the American charismatic movement
had passed through our doors. For some people, expanding to
a new location was like moving the temple to a city other than
Jerusalem. It just couldn't happen.

We prayed for months, asking God for direction, and made
sure that we were willing to obey no matter where he led us.
Because we were committed to obey, God gave us clear direction. We sensed that he was telling us to start a new church in
Red Oak, and after a time of preparation, we opened the doors at
our new facility in 2003. That first year, we averaged about 850
people at our services. We were excited about the change, but we
had only begun to see what God had in mind for us. The following year, 500 people were added to the church, and the year after
that we added *another* 500. By this time our facilities were maxed

out, and there was no room to expand. That year we grew by only 100 people. The year after that only 20 were added.

In the midst of all this, we knew that God hadn't neglected us. During our second year in the new location, we sensed God leading us to build an even larger worship center. When we began talking about this possibility, some people thought we were nuts! We still owed six million dollars on the existing building, and by all appearances we had plenty of room to grow, but the Spirit prompted us to grasp the fact that by the time our existing facilities were full, we'd need several years to build a larger building, and we'd lose all the momentum of growth. We sensed that we had to anticipate the need for more space *before* we actually needed it.

THROW A CURVE

Dr. Samuel Chand is a noted author and consultant who has helped thousands of Christian leaders reach their potential, and he has been a trusted mentor to me for several years. One of the insights Dr. Chand shared with me is a variation of something called a sigmoid curve. If you've been in ministry for more than a few years, you know that every organization, including the church, experiences natural cycles of growth and decline. The cycle typically begins with an energizing vision and moves into a growth mode. If momentum isn't sustained, the energy gradually subsides, and passion erodes into regimentation and institutionalization. Eventually the decline leads to stagnation and death. At that point, people remember the good old days when the vision was fresh and strong. The curve looks like this:

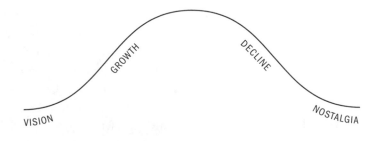

On the curve, most leaders can easily identify point B, when they notice decline and want to infuse fresh vision, strategy, and leadership into the organization. Perceptive leaders, however, notice an earlier point A, when they can take advantage of existing momentum and make adjustments before decline occurs.

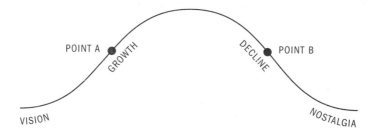

Let me be very clear about what's going on at point B, the point of stagnation and decline. The year we grew by only twenty people, our ministries were better than ever. Our worship was outstanding, our children's ministry was sensational, we saw more people saved than ever before, our youth program rocked, we were teaching and training people to become disciples more than ever before, and our leadership development program was very effective. So what was wrong? From the outside, absolutely nothing. The exceptional quality of our leadership and our programs, though, couldn't overcome the obstacles we faced. Our momentum peaked and our growth rate declined because we faced predictable, easily identifiable roadblocks: too little parking, inadequate facilities for childcare, and the 80 percent rule in our worship facility. (For those who aren't familiar with this principle, studies show that when a meeting room is 80 percent full, people perceive that there's not enough room. Even though one-fifth of the seats aren't occupied, these are often single seats. People don't feel comfortable in a room that crowded, so many of them simply leave—and many don't come back.)

If a leadership team takes action at point A and infuses the church with fresh vision, strategy, and heart, they can change the shape of the curve and experience another growth cycle.

If a leadership team takes action at point A and infuses the church with fresh vision, strategy, and heart, they can change the shape of the curve and experience another growth cycle. The time between the envisioning of the new wave at point A and the upward movement after a period of preparation (often two or three years) is full of doubt, fear, and questions.

I call it *chaos*.

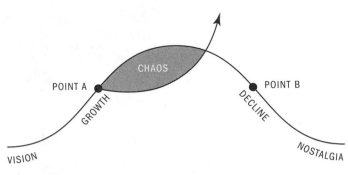

You can imagine the looks and the comments perceptive leaders get when they say, "I believe God wants us to make some major changes so we can grow," when things are going along very smoothly in the growth stage. Some people think these leaders have lost their minds, and a few followers wonder if the leader is on some kind of power trip and wants to conquer the world. Visionary leaders are, by definition, ahead of the crowd, and because they are misunderstood, people may question their motives. This is exactly what happened when God led my father and our leadership team to plant a new church in Red Oak. We were doing fine in Oak Cliff, with a rich tradition of the Spirit's work in people's lives. But God had a plan to reach more people if we'd only listen and obey. And again, it's exactly what happened in 2004 when God led us, while we were in only our second year at Red Oak and deeply in debt, to anticipate God's harvest and plan for the future. Anticipating the future enables a church to capture the existing momentum and use it in the next stage of growth. Waiting until the church begins to decline may be safer, but it forfeits time and momentum.

If a church successfully anticipates the pivot point of momentum, implements change, and moves through chaos at every point in its history, it can experience an unending chain of upward growth curves. Dr. Chand calls this pattern "glory to glory." I call it "chaos to chaos." Both are accurate appraisals of the process of capturing momentum before it declines.

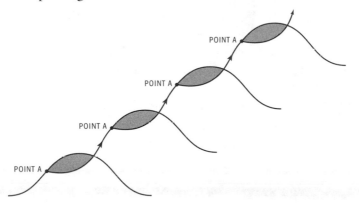

Remember, the vision isn't about buildings and budgets; it's about reaching lost people and building believers into strong men and women of faith. If we really believe that Christ died for the whole world, our hearts need to expand to care about the people he cares about. This chart isn't some kind of slick business principle to use instead of the Scriptures. It's just a way wise leaders can observe the events and trends around them.

Where does this kind of perception come from? It doesn't drop from the sky, and sadly, you can't really gain it by reading a book. A book like this can only inform you about the possibility of anticipating early pivot points of change. I believe we need to spend time with people who have been there, who have experienced chaos, and who learned to thrive in it. I look for pastors with churches that are at least three times bigger than mine. I ask to meet with them, I ask a ton of questions, I watch them cast vision, and I listen as they explain the impact of their decisions—the good ones as well as the dumb ones—so I can soak up as much as possible. If I talk to pastors who have churches only as large as ours, I enjoy their friendship, but they can't help me get to the next level. I need the wisdom of men who have walked the road before me and can speak out of their personal experience.

CHOOSING THE POINT OF CHANGE

When I communicate the principles of the curve and chaos to church leaders, the vast majority of them intuitively get it. Their eyes light up, and they smile and sigh as if they're saying, "So that's why we lost momentum. I never understood before." However, when I ask people when would be the best time to change direction and infuse the organization with a new vision for growth, while 70 percent of them say point A, 30 percent of leaders continue to say point B—the point of decline—even after I've explained the diagrams and the concepts. Those who choose point B say to me, "The problems surface at point B, so that's a good time to make a change. There's no need to change when things are going well." Those who choose to change at the later point often fail to realize that point A is the point where you *begin* the preparation phase. Leaders probably aren't going to be implementing new programs or moving into a new building for a couple of years still. But if the church waits until point B to begin preparations, all the momentum created in the growth phase is lost—and it's a lot more difficult to generate momentum than it is to capture it and use it.

THE PREPARATION PHASE OF CHAOS

If we think that everybody on our staff and in leadership in the church is going to stand up and cheer when we steer them through chaos, we're deluding ourselves. A few hardy souls may thrive on change. They love risks, and they can't wait to take the next one. The vast majority of people, however, are risk averse, especially when a transition may alter their role, which is a major part of their identity. Don't underestimate the threat of change to your people. It's not just moving names on an organizational chart. Change puts the two things they cherish most at risk: their reputation and their relationships. So the first principle about steering through chaos is to recognize that it threatens most people to the core of their being! With that realization, you'll be more patient with their resistance and more thorough in your communication. The most important elements of preparation

CHOOSING TO CHANGE
Dr. Sam Chand
Stockbridge, Georgia

Sometimes transitions are forced on us, but quite often we have the privilege—and the responsibility—to *choose* to enter the process of change. For many years I enjoyed a wonderful relationship with Beulah Heights University in Atlanta. I went to school there and worked my way through college as a janitor, cook, and dishwasher. Years later in 1989, the board asked me to come back to serve as the president of the school. For the next fourteen years, the college grew from eighty-seven students to seven hundred, and from not being accredited to receiving dual accreditation. The school was listed as one of America's fastest-growing colleges, and I found tremendous satisfaction in my role there.

By 2001, however, I began to feel restless. We weren't going through any problems with the faculty or funding that made me look for greener pastures. I just sensed a godly discontent. My solution at the time was to work harder. I hoped pouring myself into my work would make me feel more comfortable, but the sense of restlessness continued to grow. During those years, a number of leaders around the country came to me to ask for advice. Gradually I began to realize that I was more fulfilled in helping them than in my role as university president. My wife, Brenda, and I started talking about making a transition. The prospect both thrilled us and scared us. I remember waking up on many nights in excitement about the prospect of my new calling, but in cold sweats about all the unknowns. I would be leaving a stable, financially secure career in education to launch out on my own. I asked some of my friends for wise counsel, and they told me I was stupid to even consider leaving the university! Still, I felt a growing sense of "rightness" about starting my own leadership consulting firm.

Finally, on Easter Sunday in 2003, as Brenda and I drove home from church, we again talked about the possibility of a career change. She looked at me and

continued on next page…

said simply, "Let's go for it!" Immediately I realized that *how* I transitioned was just as important as *why* I was leaving. I wanted people to know that I didn't feel pushed out of my role as university president; instead I felt pulled in a new direction. I set up meetings with the board, staff, friends, and family so I could explain our reasons and our direction, and I made sure that my communication with the university staff and students came after my replacement, Dr. Benson Karanja, was confirmed.

I gave people plenty of time for a graceful transition. My last day was the end of the year, about eight months after Brenda and I made the decision. To make the shift in leadership at the university work most effectively and to give Dr. Karanja the platform he needed, I didn't set foot on the campus for nine months after I left, and even today I only go back to speak about twice a year.

Over the years, I've watched countless leaders make transitions. Sometimes they bruise people on the way out and for many years regret the pain they caused. A little thought and good planning, though, enables us to leave with grace. We may want to feel indispensable to the people we leave behind, but it's best to sever our role cleanly to honor the person who replaces us. Whether we feel pushed or pulled in a new direction, we need to carefully consider how we can make the transition with grace so that those who replace us feel affirmed and empowered.

during times of chaos are reinforcing the vision often and clearly, assessing key leadership roles, and adjusting your strategy to accomplish the purpose God has given you. Let's look at these.

Communicating Your Vision

Communicate your vision for the new wave of change *often*, *passionately*, and *with compassion*. Point people over and over again to God's heart for the lost and for believers to walk with him, and show how the new strategy will achieve those aims. If your people catch your heart for God, for those outside the church, and for them, you'll be a long way down the road in allaying fears and building enthusiasm for the future. After a while, many of us get tired of talking about the vision. We've spent countless hours thinking, praying, and dreaming, and we've talked about it with staff and board members until we're blue in the face. But vision atrophies in people's hearts and minds. If it's not constantly reinforced, they can forget why we're moving forward with a new strategy.

Paint verbal pictures for people to help them grasp what it will look like when the strategy is implemented and more people are touched by God. Explain the process of getting there, and identify the obstacles you'll face together. Through it all, impart genuine trust in God's greatness to provide and in his wisdom to lead. Fan the flames of their desire to see God honored and people reached. If you get bored with the vision, get on your knees and ask God to refresh your spirit. If your people get bored with it, ask God to give you rich, heartwarming stories of changed lives and a better way to communicate the challenge and the privilege of being used by him in others' lives.

Assessing Key Roles

A new vision prompts a fresh assessment of each staff member's role. For some, the change offers an opportunity for personal growth and greater effectiveness. But a few roles may not fit as neatly and easily in the new vision for the church. Personnel decisions are undoubtedly the hardest ones any leader has to make. Countless books have been written about managing teams, so I'm not going to dwell on this topic in detail. I want to say, though, that great leaders genuinely care for their people, and they are willing to make the hard choices to make a dream a reality.

> Personnel decisions are undoubtedly the hardest ones any leader has to make.

Years ago I heard Willow Creek Community Church pastor Bill Hybels talk about the kind of staff he looks for. He said they must be people with *character, competence,* and the ability to *connect* with others. In my experience in leading transitions, I'd add a fourth C: *capacity.* I've known some wonderful, godly staff members who worked beautifully at a certain size of ministry, but they simply didn't have the capacity to lead more people, administrate more details, and handle more complexity. When I find that I need to hire new staff, I use the same measure that I use in selecting mentors for myself: I look for people who have led ministries that are bigger than we are. If they have led larger ministries, they'll often have the vision, skills, and experience to grow their ministry at our church as well. That said, I want to be clear that we should never heartlessly discard faithful staff members because they don't have as large a capacity as we need them to have. These are usually men and women who trusted God with us, served faithfully, and deserve to be honored. In cases like this, I look for roles that fit them, and if we don't have one here, I call other pastors who might be looking for an effective staff member whose capacity fits their church's needs.

Personnel decisions have to be made all along the life cycle of an organization, but they surface more often during times of transition, when leaders assess whether current staff have the capacity to fulfill God's vision for growth. My best advice is to make people decisions very slowly. We conduct five interviews with prospective staff members, and we follow up on references so we can address the person's personal and work experiences. I may not be involved in all of the interviews, but before we hire someone, I'm at least involved in the last one. We communicate our vision and our values, and we look for a *great* fit—not just a good fit—between the person and our church's culture. If we're going to stretch ourselves to the limit to achieve all that God has called us to do, we can't settle for good enough. If a candidate doesn't fit exceptionally well, we keep looking and praying, trusting God to provide the right person at the right time.

Adjusting Your Strategy

The point of anticipating the need for growth often entails changing the strategy to enable us to pursue God's vision. We shouldn't confuse vision and strategy. Vision, calling, and values don't change. At our church (and yours too), we are called by God to reach the lost and build disciples who love him above all else. That was our calling from the first day, and it will be our calling on the last day. But our strategy to accomplish that objective changes over time as God leads us in new directions to touch more people. Vision is rock solid; strategy is flexible. Many church leaders become focused on the tangible, and they think that building the next worship center or classroom space is the vision, but a new building is only a strategy to help us do what God wants us to do. I've heard some leaders say, "God is calling us to build a new building." It may seem like a subtle distinction, but I think it's important: God hasn't called us to build buildings. He calls us to partner with him in transforming lives. Buildings are just a means to touch more people.

Vision is rock solid; strategy is flexible.

If we confuse vision and strategy, we'll rigidly cling to buildings and programs, and we'll fail to adjust our sails to go in the direction God leads us. I've watched some church leaders who thought building new buildings was their God-given vision. When the building was completed, they breathed a sigh of relief, and all the energy they had poured into the building vanished. But I've also seen people who realized that the new building was only a vehicle to fulfill God's vision. When the ribbon was cut, all the new people who attended for the first time energized the congregation, and the leaders poured their hearts into the real dream of capturing momentum and touching many lives. The difference in the two responses is remarkable and obvious.

A friend of mine—we'll call him Richard—exemplifies the principle that a church will grow only to the level of the leader's threshold for pain. A few years ago God showed him that it was time to enter the world of chaos. He anticipated the need for his church's growth, and he asked God for direction. He and his leadership team trusted God together for a clear strategy, and God gave them a wonderful sense of direction. After a few months Richard was praying about each of his staff, and he began to feel uncomfortable about one of the assistant pastors. Jake had been with him since the beginning of the church. They were great friends, and their families were very close. Jake was a wonderful man, but he let a lot of things fall through the cracks. That's not exactly the case—they didn't really fall, because Richard didn't let them fall. He often jumped in to fix problems and soothe hurt feelings caused by Jake's negligence. Now, as Richard looked at the vision God had given their church, he came face-to-face with the realization that Jake simply didn't have the capacity to be one of the key leaders. (The hard truth is that he hadn't had the capacity for his current position for many years.)

For weeks Richard prayed and asked God for wisdom. Again and again God assured him that a change had to be made. Richard was well aware of all the hurt and anger his decision would create, so he delayed the conversation with Jake again and again. Finally he called Jake and said, "Please come to my office tomorrow at two o'clock. I'd like to talk to you."

"Are you going to fire me?" Jake asked bluntly.

Richard was startled. He didn't know if the question was good news or bad news. He stammered, "Just come, and we'll talk then."

That night Richard couldn't sleep. He agonized about the conversation he would have with Jake, and he played it out over and over in his mind. He thought about how Jake's wife would respond, and he thought about all the people on staff and in the church who would accuse him of being heartless and cruel to his old friend. They wouldn't understand, and to be brutally honest, part of it was his own fault for bailing Jake out time and time again so that nobody knew his deficiencies.

The next morning Richard called Ben, the pastor of another church who had served as his mentor for several years. He told Ben about his confusion and his reluctance to meet Jake that afternoon. Ben responded, "You're not confused. You're emotionally conflicted about a very difficult decision, but you know exactly what God has called you to do. You just don't want to do it. The question is simple: Will you do what's easy, or will you follow God's leading?"

"The question is simple: Will you do what's easy, or will you follow God's leading?"

Richard asked, "But shouldn't I wait to talk to Jake when I have someone to replace him? That would make it go down easier for the people who will be upset."

Ben replied, "No, you can't wait to do God's will until you have all the bases covered and all the questions answered. Sometimes you have to take action on what you know before you find answers to what you don't know."

Ben's crystal-clear insight into the situation steeled Richard's resolve. He no longer doubted the decision or himself, so when he met with Jake, he could express genuine compassion and appreciation. When Jake protested, Richard wasn't defensive. He patiently explained his decision, and he reminded Jake of the countless times he had picked up the slack for him. After a few minutes Jake realized he couldn't argue enough to change Richard's mind, and he accepted the decision. The two men talked about how to communicate the decision so the staff and congregation could honor Jake.

The next few weeks were a time of transition for the two families and for the church as they came to grips with the staff change. As Richard had anticipated, a lot of people were upset with the decision, so for those few weeks he met with seventy-five people in the church to explain it. These people didn't understand, and many were furious. If he hadn't taken the time to talk with them, some might have left the church in anger, and for any who stayed, trust in Richard's judgment and leadership would have been severely eroded. But Richard met with everyone who wanted to meet with him, and his patience and diplomacy earned him a new level of trust from these people—all of them. Not one person left the church, and they respected Richard more than ever before.

Richard helped Jake find a position in a church in the area, and he helped Jake's family through a difficult transition. The church began conversations with candidates who might fill the vacant staff position. This moment in the church's life had been a test for Richard. Until then the principle of growing only to the threshold of pain was just a sterile concept. Suddenly it was blood, sweat, and tears. Richard almost wavered, but Ben's input had given him the clarity of thought and the strength of conviction that he needed.

As I talked to Richard about leading through chaos, he told me, "Scott, I let Jake go at point A. I could have waited until point B, when everybody in the church knew Jake couldn't do the job. But by then the energy of our church and our sense of mission would have evaporated. Jake was upset with me at point A, but he would have been just as upset with me at point B. Putting it off wouldn't have changed his attitude at all."

The shaded area on the graph earlier in this chapter is called "chaos" for a reason. It's a time when people question the reason and motives of perceptive leaders who anticipate change and begin to prepare for a new strategy. It's a lot easier to wait until everybody in the church knows change is necessary, but by then momentum is lost, and the delay prevents the church from capturing significant opportunities. Sure, chaos produces pain, but is it worth the cost? That's the question every leader has to answer for himself. The fact that a decision is difficult or unpleasant doesn't mean it's wrong. Ask God for perception, get input from a trusted mentor, and pursue God's calling with all your heart. Throughout the Scriptures, men and women who followed God paid a price of inconvenience, misunderstanding, and accusation. Should we expect anything different as we steer our way through chaos?

> Throughout the Scriptures, men and women who followed God paid a price of inconvenience, misunderstanding, and accusation.

MAPPING YOUR DIRECTION

1. Where is your church today on the sigmoid curve? Explain your answer.

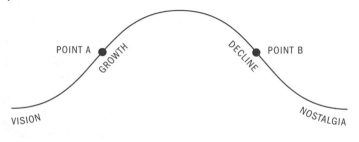

2. What does point A look like in a church's life? (What might be some characteristics of leadership, facilities, debt, programs, parking, children's ministry, and worship facilities?)

3. What does point B look like?

4. Describe a time when your church waited until point B and change was necessary. What did it feel like as you tried to lead during that transition? What were the obstacles and challenges you faced? How would it have helped if you had identified point A and begun transition then?

5. Are you and your church facing a point A decision right now? If so, describe the changes that need to occur. How do you expect people to respond to your vision for change at this point?

   What are some consequences, now and later, if you miss this opportunity and wait until point B?

6. Would you choose point A or point B to begin to change? Explain your answer.

7. How would you define and describe the shaded area of chaos?

8. As a leader, what are some specific things you must consider during the preparation phase of chaos, specifically in the following areas?

   • Communicating your vision
   • Assessing key roles
   • Adjusting your strategy

9. What are some ways in which the principle of growing to your threshold of pain shows up during times of chaos?

10. As you think about that pain, are you willing to pay that price? Why or why not?

CHAPTER 4

AUTHENTICITY

Motivating People to Follow the Vision

*Management is the process of assuring that the program
and objectives of the organization are implemented.
Leadership, on the other hand, has to do with casting
vision and motivating people.... Encouragement is the
oxygen of the soul.* — JOHN C. MAXWELL

The paradox of Christian leadership is that we live for an audience of one, and our ambition is to please him above all else, but our God-given task is to build strong relationships so that we can take people with us. As pastors, our role isn't to perform for those in our churches so they'll applaud, and it's not just to impart God's Word to them and let the truth transform lives. Certainly, teaching is a crucial component of our role, but we teach most effectively if we connect with people in a meaningful way so they really hear what we're saying.

When I was a young pastor, I saw people as cogs in the machine of ministry. I hate to admit it, but it's true. Their value was only in their ability to contribute to the success of my programs. When they had questions, I snapped answers back at them. When they didn't take action as quickly as I wanted them to respond, I wondered, "What's wrong with them? Why aren't they as committed to God as I am?" But God graciously corrected me. I realized that people aren't here to help me fulfill the vision. *They are the vision!* Everything I do is about their faith, their growth, their development, and their joy in knowing, loving, and serving God.

Leadership is built on a combination of respect and relationships. We earn people's respect by demonstrating a Christlike character—not perfection but progress in following him. We also earn respect by exercising our gifts and talents in serving God so people see we are competent to lead them. But respect without a relationship makes us authoritarians who lead by fear. That's not the model Christ demonstrated to his followers. He loved them, and they knew it. John identified himself, in his gospel, as "the disciple whom Jesus loved." Did he mean that he was the only one Jesus loved? Of course not, but the love of Jesus was so life-changing to John that it became the center of his sense of identity. In the same way, people want to know—they need to know—that we truly love them, that we're committed to their good, that we'll listen to them, that we laugh when they laugh, rejoice when they rejoice, and weep when they weep.

> People want to know—they need to know—that we truly love them, that we're committed to their good, that we'll listen to them, that we laugh when they laugh, rejoice when they rejoice, and weep when they weep.

Relationships without respect, however, don't produce effective leadership. I've known pastors who tried to be best friends with their staff, but the staff didn't respect the pastor enough to follow when he made decisions they didn't like. If pastors don't build relationships with those they lead, they lead out of fear, but if they have relationships without respect, others resent their decisions. Both are essential to good and godly leadership.

PHONINESS OR SINCERITY

Over the years, I've learned to discern phony affection in a few leaders. They smile and say they care, but they really don't. I can sense their lack of authentic love because I've been guilty of it myself. The way God corrected me when I was a young pastor was to reveal the depth of my own phoniness. I was really frustrated with people because they weren't contributing to my success as much as I demanded, so I decided to tell them that I really cared for them and see what happened. Over and over again I told people I loved them and they were my friends, but one young man confronted me. He said, "I hear your words, but I don't think you mean them."

I tried to assure him I was being honest, but in my heart I knew it was a lie. I cried out to the Lord, and he led me to a passage where he spoke through Ezekiel to condemn manipulative, selfish shepherds. This is what I read that day:

> This is what the Sovereign LORD says: Woe to the shepherds of Israel who only take care of themselves! Should not shepherds take care of the flock? You eat the curds, clothe yourselves with the wool and slaughter the choice animals, but you do not take care of the flock. You have not strengthened the weak or healed the sick or bound up the injured. You have not brought back the strays or searched for the lost. You have ruled them harshly and brutally. So they were scattered because there was no shepherd, and when they were scattered they became food for all the wild animals. My sheep wandered over all the mountains and on every high hill. They were scattered over the whole earth, and no one searched or looked for them.
>
> — EZEKIEL 34:2–6

God said, "This applies to you, Scott. If you don't change your heart, I can't use you. Don't be a general. I want you to be a shepherd."

I promised God I'd change, and that moment began a transformation of my identity as a leader. By God's grace, I began to truly care about people instead of using them for my selfish goals to achieve success. I asked the Lord for direction, and he guided me to take an important step the very next day. I gathered the people who served on my team, and I washed their feet. As I bathed them and dried them with a towel, I called their names and prayed for them, and I asked God to forgive me for not loving his people the way I should. I cried, and they cried. That act may sound silly to some people, but it was a pivotal moment in my life. I no longer thought or acted like a general commanding his troops. Now I saw myself as a shepherd, in the spirit of

Jesus with those he led, to stoop to care for them as a humble servant. My life has never been the same. I can't say that I never feel tempted to revert back to the old ways of using people, but I have established some safeguards—my wife, my mentors, and a few good friends who have the courage to say the things I really need to hear.

In this chapter, I want to address two distinct elements of shepherding people through transitions taking place in a church. One element is *proactive*; it's the need for relational touch and for a proven method to help large numbers of people buy into a vision. The other is *reactive*; it involves learning to respond constructively to the relational tensions created by changes within an organization.

BE PROACTIVE

I've known people who were awed by a leader's eloquence or vision, and they followed because they wanted to be part of something big. That works for some people some of the time, but it doesn't have sustaining power. A number of people have told me with tears in their eyes that they were attracted to a leader because of his exemplary gifts, but his lack of love sooner or later caused them to doubt his leadership and lose respect for him as a person. Instead we need to look to the Master, the one who never took his eyes off the goal but who tenderly, patiently, and lovingly cared for the men and women who followed him. He was the one whose face was set "like flint" toward Jerusalem and death but who touched lepers, stopped to spend time with snotty children, went out of his way to show love to outcasts, and valued women in a male-dominated society. Respect and relationship—that's Jesus' leadership model. He was the consummate example of a leader who connected with people through relational touch.

Relational Touch

As churches prepare for transition, people often feel afraid of and disoriented by the impending changes. They wonder what their new role will be, and when they find out, they wonder if they'll be able to fulfill it. Staff members, board members, and top lay leaders are usually the ones most directly affected, but whenever you talk about making changes in the children's or youth ministry, you can bet that parents will start acting like mama bears taking care of their cubs. They can get very feisty! Sometimes they don't want to talk about the things that really concern them — that's too frightening — so they speak in anger about things that seem to come out of nowhere. Whenever a person's reaction is disproportionate or displaced, you can be sure there's a volcano ready to blow.

When the organizational stress is at its highest, leaders need to make sure they take time to connect with people in meaningful ways. In Psalm 23, David says that a shepherd uses a rod and a staff to comfort his sheep and provide relational touch. He uses the rod to fend off wolves and any other predators, and he uses the crook of his staff to draw the sheep near him. I believe God has given pastors the tools of shepherding for the very same reasons, to protect our flocks and draw them near to us. Relational touch is *essential* in times of transition and chaos. We need to look beyond the fearful and angry reactions we see and provide comfort and reassurance.

It's not enough to stand up on a Sunday morning and say, "I love you. You're the greatest. We're going to get through this time together." We need to target the key influencers in the church, individuals whose roles might be changing, who may be the most fearful and anxious, and whose attitudes have the potential to affect other people. A shepherd's staff only works effectively on one sheep at a time, and we need to spend time with these key leaders individually. Yes, this takes a lot of time, and yes, I know you have lots of things to do — but relational touch is essential. When we moved from Oak Cliff to Red Oak, I made a list of the top one hundred influencers in the church, and I made an appointment to see every one of them. In each meeting, I made an assumption: they were interested in the big picture, but they really wanted to know how the transition specifically affected them. If I hadn't addressed that concern, I would have made a colossal mistake.

Invest the time and energy in breakfasts, lunches, dinners, coffees, golf games, and any other way you can effectively connect with the leaders of your church to share your heart, impart your vision, explain the strategy, and tell how the change will affect them. But don't just perform a data dump on them. Listen. Invite questions, and don't give your answers too quickly. Instead ask follow-up questions to make sure people feel heard and understood. That's your primary goal in these meetings. Even if people don't completely agree with every detail of the plan, most of them will be supportive if—and only if—they believe you've heard and understood their concerns. When your staff and lay leaders feel loved, understood, and appreciated during times of chaos, they'll support you and the vision for change.

Sometimes a transition will affect a large group of people, and it may be helpful to pull them all together to communicate the process of change. During our latest transition, we decided to make a sweeping change in Christian education. We no longer had space for our traditional Sunday school classes. When I told the Sunday school teachers about the change, their mental filter translated my words into, "Your teaching gift isn't important to the church or to me anymore." Now, that's the farthest thing from the truth, but this was their perception. I asked them to pray with me for two weeks to ask God for wisdom about how we—the teachers and the pastoral staff—could accomplish God's purposes to equip people better than ever. By asking the teachers to pray and think, I made them a part of the process. A few weeks later God gave us a vision of how these teachers could use their gifts in a different way to have an impact far beyond the walls of our church, by teaching and training with a video curriculum so people all over the world could be equipped to follow Christ and advance his kingdom! Since the teachers were involved in the process and understood the vision, their former despair was turned into excitement.

Cascading Communication

As we've already talked about, our task as leaders is to pursue God with our whole hearts to get his vision for our churches. We want to learn from everyone who can teach us, but ultimately we need a vision with God's stamp on it. The vision is formed by examining our gifts, our passions, and the needs of our community. Our staff and board wrestled with the questions in chapter 2 for weeks, if not months. We took nothing for granted. Instead we kept probing, doing research, asking questions, and praying until we were convinced that we had grasped the essential elements of God's vision for our church. We don't always look for unanimity in our decisions, but in matters of major importance — the choices that affect our overall direction, vision, and strategy as a church — we won't proceed until every person on the staff and

> The vision is formed by examining our gifts, our passions, and the needs of our community.

COMMUNICATING CHANGE

Tim Stevens
Granger Community Church: Granger, Indiana

Within the first few months after taking office, President Obama held a town hall meeting a few minutes away from our church. He announced to the watching world that he was standing in the county with the worst unemployment rate in the nation. That wasn't a surprise to us in Granger — we had been feeling the pain of the downward-spiraling economy for nearly two years.

In fact, the economic challenges led us to the agonizing decision to cut eight full-time staff positions. We could no longer afford to pay people on our staff. That meant I had to fire a woman who had served us faithfully for more than ten years, another who is a single mom with three kids, another whose mother-in-law died the night before, and another who was my personal assistant and good friend.

I've long believed that it's not bad decisions that cause leaders to fail; more often than not it's bad communication. Very few leaders fail because they make the wrong decisions. But many fail because they don't take the time to communicate their decision to the right people, at the right time, and in the right order. In my experience, I'd say 20 percent of leadership is making the right decisions. Eighty percent is appropriately communicating those decisions.

continued on next page…

And appropriate communication was needed for this transition. We had people who walked into work on a Monday morning with a job and left minutes later unemployed. We had remaining staff members who had just learned they would no longer be working with their best friend. We had family members who were hurting for their dad or mom or spouse. We had eight people whom we loved and cherished now entering a job climate that was harsh—where one in six people were unemployed and looking for work. We had volunteers who were rightfully in pain for their friends.

Challenging leadership transitions require great communication. But communication isn't an exact science. It requires strategy, assessment, execution, reassessment, more execution, and finally evaluation of what worked and what didn't. I'm not a pro at this, but I have learned a few things in my fifteen years at Granger:

- Start with a written communication strategy.
- Don't delay your communication. Waiting says you are hiding something.
- Consider your key influencers. Who needs to know first? Then who? Who after that?
- Be straight with people. No one will be surprised that you are facing troubles. They are just watching to see how you will handle it.
- Ask people to help you. Everyone has potential to fuel the fire of gossip and bitterness or put it out. Call your leaders to be firefighters for a short time, and provide them water (i.e., information) so they can be effective.
- Plan time for conversations to help people process. You've been living in the pain for a while and are ready to move on. But they are experiencing it for the first time. Give them space to vent.

If you aren't going through a tough transition right now, I can promise you that one is just around the corner. Spend time making the best decision you possibly can with the information you have available. But then spend most of your time focusing on communication. That is where the battle is won or lost.

the board are in broad agreement that this is indeed God's leading for us as a church.

Once our vision and values were clear, we began the long process of informing our key leaders and volunteers and enlisting their support. I met with all of our key donors one-on-one to share my heart and the specifics of the strategy. I didn't ask them for money. That would come later. I first wanted them to catch God's heart and grasp the vision. These people are sharp. They're not satisfied with a lot of lofty words about what God might do. They want to know the exact strategy that will achieve those aims. Without a sound strategy, the vision is just hype, no matter how well it's communicated.

> Without a sound strategy, the vision is just hype, no matter how well it's communicated.

We scheduled a meeting with our top tier of lay leaders in the church—teachers, administrators, and other ministry leaders—about two hundred people altogether. I asked the staff, the board, and some of our key donors to join us, and as I shared the vision with this tier of leaders, those who were already on board nodded their hearty approval. We answered every question people had, and we honored them for asking.

Next we scheduled a meeting with all of our volunteer leaders, from childcare to greeters to small group leaders to everybody who served in any capacity at the church—about six hundred people. I asked the staff, board, key donors, and top tier of lay leaders to come to this meeting, and as I explained the vision and strategy, all those who had been in previous meetings nodded in agreement. When all of our leaders are informed and enthused—and only then—we share the vision with the rest of the congregation.

CASCADING COMMUNICATION

STAFF AND BOARD

TOP LAY LEADERS

ALL VOLUNTEERS

THE ENTIRE CONGREGATION

If you put dates next to each audience on the chart, you'll have an effective plan for communicating your vision to the church, earning each group's buy-in and enlisting their support as you share with the next group. This strategy of communicating a fresh, challenging direction to a congregation builds momentum from one group to the next, capturing the enthusiasm of each group as the vision is shared with the next one. As more and more leaders get on board, I often ask particular people to share their excitement about the vision and how the changes will affect their ministry area. Then people will see that a host of leaders at our church are trusting God together for direction. We've wrestled with hard questions, we've debated the solutions, and we're glad to talk about any aspect of it, because we really want every person to feel the excitement we feel about God's calling. I call this momentum-building process of meeting with groups "cascading communication."

Does cascading the communication of vision take time and energy? Yes, it consumes a lot of both, but I believe it's well worth every second and every drop of sweat. It's the best way I've ever found to capture hearts, allay fears, and enlist support for a new direction. Think of the anguish and heartache caused by leaders who assume that all they need to do is announce their vision to the congregation. If they think that people will meekly fall in line, they'll be very defensive when people ask questions—even very logical ones that aren't full of doubt and fear. These pastors are asking for trouble!

Make wise assumptions as you plan to communicate vision to your people. It's foolish to think that people should fall in line without asking any questions and without any fear of change. Most people dread change like the plague! In counseling, the first goal of the counselor is for the client to feel understood. Likewise, in communicating vision, the first goal of the pastor is for his people to feel he understands and cares for them. If they know that he loves them and that he has pursued God with his whole heart, and if they believe that a host of top leaders have wrestled with the implications of change, they may still have questions, and they'll still feel afraid of what it will mean to them—but it won't take as long for them to trust that God is in it.

Moving in a new direction won't affect some people very much at all. But for others, it turns their world completely upside down. When a cherished role is no longer needed, or friendships are changed because reporting structures are altered, people need sufficient time to adjust. They feel a sense of loss, and they need some time to grieve.

Don't expect people to jump on the train six minutes after you've talked with them, when it's taken you six months to get moving. Be a good shepherd. Be patient, understanding, gracious, and loving. Even people who aren't asking questions are watching to see how you respond to those who have the guts to ask. Let them see you at your best, earning respect as you genuinely care for them.

WHEN YOU HAVE TO BE REACTIVE, DON'T IGNORE RELATIONAL TENSION

Make no mistake: leadership can be incredibly lonely. Even if you have a wonderful mentor and your spouse thinks you're Superman without the cape and tights, you will, like every leader, face resistance to innovative ideas. With the support of a mentor and a few close friends, you'll be able to learn and grow during those times in the desert, but without that support, most of us are as easy to live with as a porcupine in a sleeping bag! There are times when every move people make, whether toward us or away from us, results in more hurt and pain. But it doesn't have to be that way. If we try to protect ourselves by withdrawing or blaming, we short-circuit the redemptive potential of every relationship. The main principle for dealing with the inevitable conflicts that arise from visionary leadership is this: don't ignore relational tension. Let me give you a few principles that guide our responses to disagreement and conflict.

Make Relational Touch a Priority before Transitions Occur

In times of change, people get upset, confused, anxious, and angry. It's a given. However, if I've built relationships of trust and understanding before we enter chaos, we'll have a strong foundation of love and respect, and little problems won't become major bombs. So the first principle of reactive response is to proactively create strong relationships. Love covers a multitude of sins, and it prevents a lot of transitional problems too.

Love covers a multitude of sins, and it prevents a lot of transitional problems too.

I know a pastor who recently had two major explosions on his elder board. On both occasions men left the church (and one took a fourth of the church with him) because relatively small problems in their relationships with the pastor weren't addressed years ago. The lack of trust between these men and the pastor was never resolved, so disappointment became suspicion, and suspicion turned into the conviction that the pastor was a selfish, manipulative leader. Individually these men accused the pastor in front of the elder board, and their now-hardened perceptions couldn't be changed by reason. They felt betrayed and abandoned, and they were furious. Their response was completely out of line with the original problems, but those difficulties were never addressed, and trust was never rebuilt. Gradually the relationships became toxic, and everyone suffered. In both cases the problem surely wasn't only the pastor's fault, but for years he never invested in relational touch with these men — or anybody else, for that matter.

Implement an Honesty Policy

At our church, we are radically committed to resolving problems while they are still manageable, before they go subterranean and escalate into major blowups. Jesus gave a simple direction: "If your brother sins against you, go and show him his fault, just between the two of you. If he listens to you, you have won your brother over" (Matt. 18:15). We've implemented an honesty policy that has worked very well. First we drafted a statement, and we asked each staff and board member to agree to it. We then had this statement printed and framed so each of us could see it every day to remind us.

Honesty Policy

I promise to speak the truth in love to all the people around me. I will not gossip. If I have a problem in my heart toward someone, I will go to them personally and promptly so we might be reconciled to each other and maintain unity in accordance with Matthew 18:15. I will speak the whole truth to others, even to the last 10 percent, knowing that it's the whole truth that will make the difference.

During times of relational tension, people are usually willing to say 90 percent of what they need to say, but they feel very uncomfortable with the last 10 percent. This part has the most potential for hurt, but it also holds the most potential for genuine change. A friend of mine told me about a seemingly innocuous tension with a deacon at his church. This man had served for several years, and in virtually every deacon's meeting he voiced a negative opinion about whatever topic was being addressed. In the first few months, the pastor excused the behavior and thought, "He's just having a bad day. He'll come around." But he didn't. After a year or so the pastor had lunch with the deacon and said, "You know, it would be good if you could find something positive to share with the group. It would really help us. I appreciate your observations, though. Don't get me wrong." He had a golden opportunity to speak the whole truth, but he chickened out.

The negative perceptions kept rolling from the deacon's lips. Soon the pastor started avoiding the man, not giving him eye contact at church, walking the other way in the hall, and finding someone else to talk to whenever this deacon was around. Avoiding the issue, though, wasn't solving anything. The pastor tried correcting him a couple of times, but both times his gentle request was either misunderstood or rejected. This deacon's behavior absorbed far too much of the pastor's thoughts, and to be honest, genuine resentment began to build in the pastor's heart. He dreaded deacon's meetings, simply because this man was there.

Finally the pastor realized he needed to lance the boil. He met with the deacon, and this time he didn't stop at 50 percent or 90 percent. He told him, "I appreciate your gifts of analysis, but I need you to understand the impact your negative perspective is having on me, the deacons, and the church." The pastor gave him chapter-and-verse examples, and then he said, "Brother, this has to change." The deacon was instantly defensive, but that's to be expected in any confrontation. The pastor, to his credit, didn't react. Instead he asked, "Tell me what this is about. I didn't see you as a negative person before we asked you to be a deacon." At that point the man began to unfold his life's story. He was from an alcoholic family, and he had a long history of distrust of authority. This conversation was the beginning of healing long-buried wounds in the deacon's life, and the start of a rich, rewarding relationship between the two men. None of that had been possible when the pastor was only willing to speak 90 percent of the truth. The Spirit was free to work only when he was willing to be totally honest and blend brutal truth with heartfelt grace.

Continually Cultivate Connections

When we drive past a beautifully manicured lawn with immaculate flowers, we don't assume it just happened. Somebody worked hard to till the soil, plant, water, fertilize, weed, prune, and mow so it would be the showpiece of the neighborhood. Sometimes people tell our staff that we have the best relationships of any staff team they've ever seen, but they don't see how hard we've worked to cultivate our relationships.

In Psalm 133, David wrote, "How good and pleasant it is when brothers live together in unity!" But this kind of unity is the result of each person's devotion to Christ and to a common cause. Paul wrote his letter to the Ephesians as the grand declaration of the purpose and function of the church. At the beginning of the application section of this letter, Paul instructs them (and us): "As a prisoner for the Lord, then, I urge you to live a life worthy of the calling you have received. Be completely humble and gentle; be patient, bearing with one another in love.

Make every effort to keep the unity of the Spirit through the bond of peace" (Eph. 4:1 – 3). Relationships, like lawns, gardens, and every other created thing, suffer from entropy, the tendency toward decay and disorder. We need to continually cultivate our most cherished relationships through spending unrushed time together, showing honesty, performing acts of love, speaking affirming words, and celebrating each other's successes.

To keep a lawn or flowerbed beautiful, gardeners have to pluck out the weeds whenever they arise, and they're always looking for weeds to pull. When it comes to relationships, I'm a weed puller. As I've already shared, we conclude our staff meetings with me going around the room asking each person questions like, "Is there anything we need to talk about?" "Any questions or hurts you want to voice?" "Are we okay?" This exercise communicates that I place a high value on honesty and communication, and God uses this time to clear the air whenever there's a problem brewing.

> When it comes to relationships, I'm a weed puller.

Let Love Reign

I'm sure it grieves God's heart when staff teams, elder boards, and ministry leaders pour out so much effort in ministry but resent one another personally. In one of the most familiar passages in the New Testament, Paul reminds us that no amount of speaking in tongues, prophesying, faith, generosity, or sacrifice can substitute for genuine love. Jesus showed us "the full extent of his love" (John 13:1) by dying for us. He didn't just tolerate us; he looked at our worst sins and our selfish hearts, and he still loved us. That's the marvel of God's grace, and when we go out of our way to care for one another, people will marvel at the grace of God being expressed in our relationships. Do people really notice the way we treat each other? You bet they do! As the Scriptures remind us, this is how people will know we are Jesus' disciples — by the way we love one another.

Relationships are incredibly fragile. It takes only one unresolved hurt to fester into suspicion and vain thoughts that nurse the hurt and seek revenge. Before long the unity of the Spirit has been eroded by distrust or shattered by anger. When we choose to love, serve, and give to one another, to resolve disputes and overlook petty disagreements, we can pursue God together and live in the unity of the Spirit.

The leader's role — especially during periods of transition — isn't to demand loyalty and affection from his followers but to point people to Christ as the head of the church. Together, leaders and those who follow them look to God for direction, encouragement, and strength. And together they sharpen their desire to please him as they listen to one another and learn valuable lessons from each other. Unity doesn't necessarily mean that everybody agrees on every detail, but it certainly means that each person pursues God, respects others, listens well, resolves any conflicts, and lives for a cause bigger than their own comfort.

Realize the Cost of Delay

Years ago an ad for oil filters had a tough mechanic look at the camera and say, "You can pay me now, or you can pay me later." The same principle applies in many areas of life, especially in dealing with disagreements, hurts, misunderstandings, and conflicts. Nobody enjoys talking about these things. Avoiding them provides the short-term benefit of relief, but in the long run it often costs far more in time, energy, and heartache.

When there is a vacuum in our communication with others, the enemy of our souls has a field day. He feeds our minds with doubts about the other person, and he gives us a hundred excuses not to resolve the problem. Unresolved hurts don't just go away, and contrary to popular thinking, time doesn't heal all wounds. If hurt and anger aren't addressed, people may develop a victim mentality in which they believe that others are out to get them and in which they are easily offended by our words and actions, regardless of our intentions. At this point in a relationship, though the original offense might be a million miles away, possibly even forgotten, every new day brings fresh wounds to the person who thinks they are a victim.

As you read these past few sentences, you may have realized that this describes you right now. Perhaps there is someone who has hurt you whom you have yet to forgive, a person you've been avoiding because of a disagreement that happened last week, last year, or a decade ago. Don't wait any longer. Go to that person and let them know that there's something you want to talk about with them. Be honest, and look for the common ground of understanding, but clearly explain how they have hurt you. You may find that the person responds graciously and asks for your forgiveness, but let's be honest—many people are so defensive that they can't (or won't) admit they were wrong in any way. Regardless of the person's response, know that you've done what you needed to do. Paul's statement to the Romans is realistic: "If it is possible, as far as it depends on you, live at peace with everyone" (Rom. 12:18). Sadly, not everyone will respond with truth and grace.

As you've been reading these words, the Spirit may have also reminded you that someone has something against *you* because of hurtful things you have said or something you have done. Jesus' directive is equally clear in this situation. Stop what you're doing and go to that person to ask for forgiveness. Make restitution if necessary and begin to rebuild trust by practicing honesty and integrity (see Matt. 5:23–24).

THE MATRIX OF STRESS

One pastor reported, "No matter how well our church is doing, I live with a certain level of low-grade disappointment in myself and my leadership." If we expect everybody to stand up and cheer every time we enter a room, we're going to be very surprised! Even in the best of times, a small percentage of people will criticize the pastor. I don't know if they have a problem with authority, if they wake up grumpy each morning, or if their dog died last night, but they will find fault in everything you do. In addition to the normal stresses of being in the ministry, times of transition and chaos multiply stress. We not only have to keep doing the things we've always done, but now we have to manage the process of change. Every person who is affected by the change (and that's everybody) feels anxious about it and needs our time to talk about it and be reassured that things will be okay.

During times of change and transition, you shouldn't expect to keep carrying your regular workload and then pile on the added workload of the transition. It will probably be too much to handle. In every situation, regardless of our circumstances, we should be able to minister with joy in our hearts and a song on our lips. Even though transitions are challenging, we can't afford to cave in to the temptation to become a grumbler. People are reading our body language as well as listening to our words, and they take their cues from the vibes we give off.

Frequently you'll find that it's right in the midst of the hardest and most difficult transitions that the car breaks down, a child breaks a leg, you get sick, the pipes burst at the house, or your mother-in-law comes for a visit. Pastors who love to shepherd their people are often sensitive people who care deeply, but are not always the most gifted administrators and take criticism very personally. This matrix of stress—physical, emotional, and relational—forms a perfect storm for a senior pastor. At these times of maximum tension, we're tempted to cocoon—withdrawing from people, blaming them for the pressure, and ratcheting back our vision to something more manageable because we conclude, "It's just not worth it."

When the matrix of stress threatens to overwhelm you—and I assure you it will if you ask God for his vision and lead through chaos—I encourage you to do four things.

1. *Find a mentor who can give you encouragement and perspective.* Meet with them on a consistent basis so you can process the difficult decisions you are facing and maintain emotional health. This is not a time to lead alone.

You need someone who can act as a sounding board and a dumping ground for some of the raw feelings you are experiencing.

2. *Take time to create an organizational structure so you can delegate to competent people.* It's not enough to just give work away; you must be confident that the people and the structure you've put in place can handle the job. When you assign a task, you should be able to unload the emotional stress that goes along with it.

3. *Carve out time to recharge your batteries for thirty minutes every day and a full day every week.* There will always be more to do than time to get it done. Know that, and learn to live with it. You may be able to gut it out and lead on sheer willpower for a while, but not for long. Sooner or later you'll crash, and you won't have the energy to lead a Little League team, much less a band of volunteers and staff who are trying to storm the gates of hell for Christ!

4. *Prioritize your relationships.* Unless your church is very small, you simply can't be available for everybody all the time. Make sure you spend time with God, your spouse, and your children. That's not negotiable. Of course, you'll have to be flexible sometimes, but you have to guard the passions of your heart and your relationships with the dearest people in your life. If those sink, your joy and your authority to lead are shot.

If we let stress suffocate our lives, we can easily miss out on God's desire to use us in unusual ways. If we remain sharp, however, we will be constantly aware of the opportunities that God brings into our lives every day.

TAKING TIME FOR GOD'S INTERRUPTIONS

A few years ago a tall, trim, older gentleman walked into the office of Richard Miller, one of our staff members. He introduced himself and explained why he'd come. "I'm Al Swingle. I've traveled a great deal in my life, and to be honest, I've had a charmed life. A friend told me about a mission trip your church is planning to help people in a little village in Mexico, and I'd like to know if I can go."

As Richard asked Al some questions, he was surprised by some of the answers. Richard asked Al about his relationship with God, but Al shot back, "I really don't believe in God at all, and I certainly don't believe in the resurrection. Can you deal with that?" To his credit, Richard wasn't put off by Al's blunt answer. Al went on to explain that he had recently retired from a position with the Army and Air Force Exchange Service, a job that had given him plenty of opportunities to travel and paid him a good salary—the source of his "charmed life." Now, in the twilight of his life, he just wanted to do something for others. At the end of the conversation, Richard explained to Al that a group from the church would be going on a mission trip to tell people about Jesus. "If you want to go," Richard said, "you're more than welcome."

One of our pastors, Mark Brewer, has taught our staff that it takes an average of seventeen conversations with eleven different people before a person is ready to receive Christ. While that's certainly not a magical formula for evangelism, it is a constant reminder to our staff that it often takes patience and people to bring someone to the Lord. After Al's visit that day, Richard began making a list of eleven people he could connect him with. Richard put his own name at the top of the list and made a commitment to have seven conversations with Al about Christ. He expected that the other ten people on the list would talk with Al at least once. Shortly after Al walked out of his office, Richard got on the phone and lined up the other people.

Before leaving on the trip, Al began to study some books about Jesus, including the Bible. He started attending Sunday morning services at the Oaks Fellowship, and he was very attentive during the messages. He was soaking it all in!

Richard met with Al several times before the mission trip, and they had wonderful conversations about Christ. Al had been studying the books in detail, taking notes and jotting down questions to ask Richard. In one of these talks on a Saturday night,

Richard felt the prompting of the Holy Spirit to tell Al that he had studied enough for now, and that God has given each of us the measure of faith that it takes to believe in Jesus. Richard closed the books on the table and told him, "When you go to bed tonight, before you go to sleep, just stretch your arms toward heaven and say, 'God, I don't know how it all works, but whatever you do in people, do it in me. I invite you into my life.' "

At church the next morning, Al walked up to Richard with a big smile on his face. He jokingly said, "I did what you told me to do last night, and I don't recommend you ever tell anyone to do that again." He said he was still wide awake at 3:00 a.m. because God was doing something in him. He was finding out that Christ was real!

The mission trip ended up being a fantastic experience for Al. In fact, he enjoyed it so much that he went on two additional trips as well. These trips have helped Al to grow in his faith, opening his eyes to a reality that he had never considered before. Recently Al and five other men went with Richard on a four-day reunion tour of several border towns in Mexico, visiting some of the places where they had ministered on previous trips. They went to the home of a man named Mario, a very dangerous and imposing figure. The people of the village were quite certain that Mario was demon-possessed. In fact, they forced him to live in a specially made iron cell built in his mother's house for his own safety — as well as the safety of everyone else. He was known to throw feces on people who visited him, and he would try to kill anyone he could get his hands on. During a previous trip, Richard and the team had prayed for Mario for more than two hours. And God had responded to their prayers. Mario's condition had shown constant improvement, and he had been released from his cell after three weeks of observation. Standing in Mario's empty cell and witnessing the evident change in his life, Al turned to Richard and said, "Now I believe God can do miracles."

I share this story for a reason. Can you picture what would have happened if someone like Al had walked into the office of a stressed-out staff member? Instead of extending grace and seeing an opportunity for God to work, a stressed-out pastor or church leader might have looked at the old man as an unwelcome intrusion: "You want to go on a mission trip. Well, you're too old. And besides, you're not even a Christian! Call my secretary after you've come to Christ. We'll see what we can do." Thankfully, Richard didn't respond that way at all. Because he was focused and aware, living within appropriate boundaries, he was able to extend God's grace.

REMEMBER JESUS

Nobody ever said it was easy to be a shepherd. God hasn't called pastors to be field marshals or architects. The responsibility of pastoring is often just as challenging and complex, but our role deals primarily with people, not weapons or buildings. When we consider the weight of pressure that comes during times of transition, it can be tempting to feel sorry for ourselves. "Nobody understands me," we might moan. "I'm in this all alone." But that's not really true. Even when no one around us fully grasps the weight of responsibility we shoulder, there is always one person who does: Jesus.

When I get discouraged, I think about the pressure Jesus experienced and how he was able to continue loving people through it. Even from the beginning of his ministry, Jesus was haunted by the reality of his eventual death. In everything he did, Jesus lived with the awareness that he had come to die and that the events of his life would eventually lead him to the suffering of the cross. He called a dozen men to follow him, knowing one would betray him. The rest of his followers weren't much better. They consistently misunderstood his teaching, and they failed to grasp the purpose of his life. Even though they saw him heal the sick, raise the dead, and confound the religious leaders, they were still slow to recognize his true identity. But Jesus seldom criticized them. He was patient with their failures and mistakes. Though I can't know this with certainty, I can imagine him laughing and talking with his disciples around countless campfires, sharing meals with them on the dirt-floor homes of the villages of Palestine.

Though Jesus' followers were so slow to grasp his vision, they were absolutely convinced that he loved them. Though they argued about who would be the greatest, Jesus graciously forgave them, fed them, appeared to them over a period of forty days after the resurrection, and entrusted to them the task of carrying forward the single greatest endeavor in history.

> Though Jesus' followers were so slow to grasp his vision, they were absolutely convinced that he loved them.

If Jesus was able to exhibit patience while bearing the weight of such a great responsibility, perhaps I can be a little more patient with my people. If Jesus was willing to put up with those who were slow to understand and was willing to take the time to communicate his heart a hundred times, maybe I can find time to share the vision once more too. If Jesus kept loving and caring for people even while living under intense stress, maybe I can reach out to touch the people around me when I feel pressured.

Remember, God's vision isn't about numbers or buildings; it's about people. The people you and I see every day—the people Jesus died for. As we take strides to fulfill God's calling, we need to keep in mind that no matter how difficult people can be, they aren't the obstacles to reaching the vision—they *are* the vision.

MAPPING YOUR DIRECTION

1. Have you ever served under someone whose statements of devotion to Christ and of love for people seemed phony? How did you respond?

2. How would your best friends say you're doing on the phoniness-sincerity scale? Explain your answer.

3. Describe someone who demonstrated a high degree of relational touch. How did people respond to that person?

4. If you and your church are beginning or in the middle of a transition, write a brief plan for cascading communication.

How do you think this will help people get on board with the vision?

5. Evaluate your current status in responding to conflict in the following areas, and write one idea of what you can do better in each one.

    - Make relational touch a priority before transitions occur
    - Implement an honesty policy
    - Continually cultivate connections
    - Let love reign
    - Realize the cost of delay

6. What are two things you can do right now to handle the matrix of stress more effectively?

7. Who are the top key influencers in your church or ministry?

    How are you proactively communicating appreciation and love to them?

    What plan or system have you created to consistently stay in contact with these key influencers?

CHAPTER 5

CORPORATE PRAYER

Trusting God Together

The condition of the church may be very accurately gauged by its prayer meetings. So the prayer meeting is a grace-ometer, and from it we may judge of the amount of divine working among a people. If God be near a church, it must pray. And if He be not there, one of the first tokens of His absence will be a slothfulness in prayer! — CHARLES HADDON SPURGEON

A bold vision generates a lot of enthusiasm, but sooner or later the reality of chaos sets in, and we feel overwhelmed. When the multitude of seemingly insurmountable challenges — personal, organizational, and financial — forces us to our knees, we are wise to seek the company of trusted friends. Point A on the sigmoid curve isn't just a theory for our church. When we got to that point and saw that we needed to take steps of faith that would anticipate growth, we knew that steering through this time of chaos wouldn't be easy. I didn't want to force anybody to take those steps. While I'm certainly willing to lead others, I wanted to be sure we were following God's direction, and I wanted all of us to follow that direction *together*.

Prayer meetings are one of those things that every pastor knows he should be doing. But we don't schedule prayer meetings so we can check it off our list of good things we ought to do. The goal of corporate prayer is creating an environment in which believers can genuinely pursue God with one heart, one mind, and one voice. We need to move beyond the perfunctory to the profound.

HARD QUESTIONS, NECESSARY ANSWERS

When our church received the vision to reach more people in our community, we were at a point where we still owed quite a bit of money on the building we had moved into just a few years earlier. Now we felt that God was directing us to build an eighteen million dollar new facility. As we looked back at the history of our church, we knew that we had a track record of consistently trusting God and seeing him meet our needs. When we moved into the building in Red Oak, our projections showed that we would fall ten thousand dollars short each month on our offerings. Instead we found that our people gave even more than was needed.

> We needed God to speak to all the leaders of the church so that his direction was unmistakable.

From that first Sunday, God provided. Still, that was a six-million-dollar loan. This new building would require three times as many financial resources. Could we expect God to provide again? Would we be testing him? We couldn't afford to make this decision based on business principles or common sense. And we certainly couldn't rely upon the leading of God sensed by a single person, no matter who they were. We needed God to speak to all the leaders of the church so that his direction was unmistakable.

For a year we had made preliminary plans to move ahead with the building. We talked about what growth might look like, and we began to anticipate the myriad of decisions we'd have to make. Finally the board gave us the go-ahead to hire an architect to make some drawings and give us an estimate of the cost. Weeks later he came back with the drawings. They looked great! Then he showed us the projected costs. Suddenly enthusiasm vanished like air going out of a balloon. Members of the board shook their heads and moaned:

> "Can we afford eighteen million dollars? We haven't paid off the first building yet."
> "That's impossible."
> "Pastor, that's outside our reach."
> "It looks foolish to me to commit ourselves to this kind of debt."

The implication of all these comments was, "Are you insane?"

No, I'm not insane. In fact, I was as cautious and anxious as any of them. I certainly didn't want to incur an additional eighteen million dollars in debt unless this was the clear, unmistakable directive of the Lord. And I wasn't going to move ahead without the Spirit confirming his leading in all of our hearts. "Gentlemen," I told them, "we're going to trust God to lead us, and if he leads us to move ahead, it's foolish for us to disobey."

This conversation occurred in our board meeting on Thursday night. Before we left the room, I told them to pray, fast, study the Scriptures, and do whatever it takes for them to hear from God. "We're going to meet after church next Wednesday night, and I want to hear from each of you then."

We met in my office the next Wednesday night. I prayed, and then I asked them a single question: "Are we ready to do whatever God leads us to do?" I asked this question because if we weren't open to the Spirit from the beginning, all of our discussions and debates would be worthless. I looked at each person in the room, and each one said, "Yes, I'm ready."

Then I asked, "Did God speak to you about our direction? Tell us what he said and how he told you." We went around the room. One man said, "I was reading a passage of Scripture, and the Lord showed me that we need to trust him and move ahead with this project." Another man said, "On Sunday morning I was praying, and God impressed a message on my heart: 'Don't fear. Don't shrink back from this opportunity.' I believe he wants us to move forward." Five board members said that God had told them clearly that we needed to trust him and take steps of faith. Then I asked the four silent members what God had said to them. One after another, they all said something like, "I don't know. God hasn't said anything to me."

After the last one finished, I told the group. "Men, God isn't confused. He knows exactly what he wants us to do, so why haven't we all heard from him yet?"

One of the silent men answered, "Maybe we didn't have time to really hear from God."

"I understand," I told him. "All of us are busy. But men, we are the elders of the church. We are responsible to lead the people of the Oaks Fellowship. Do you know what that means? It means that we hear from God! That's our task, that's our privilege, and that's what we must do if we are going to lead this church. If you have to stay up all night so that you hear from him, stay up. If you have to fast for a week to hear from him, do whatever it takes. But don't tell the group that you don't know God's leading when you haven't made pursuing him a priority."

The men who came without a word from God agreed that they hadn't made it a high priority. I told them, "Next week we're going to meet again after church on Wednesday night, and I trust you'll have heard from God so you can share with us that night. We all need to hear from God on this, so next week come prepared to share the word God gave you and how he revealed it to you."

I explained the reason why I was so adamant about the need for all of us to hear from God: "Gentlemen, there will be times when we run into obstacles. We may run out of money, and we may run behind schedule. People will criticize us, and we may doubt ourselves. In all of these difficulties, we'll have only one thing to keep us going: together and individually, the people in this room heard clearly from God, and we must obey him. We're not going to move ahead on a five-to-four vote. If we did that, a year from now when we hit those obstacles, some of you would point at me and say, 'Pastor, you got us into this.' No, we're not moving forward until we can all say that God got us into this. It's his leading. We're just following." That night we all committed to each other to do whatever it might take to hear the still, small voice of God.

The next Wednesday night after our service, the members of our board filed into my office again. And again I went around the room to ask if and how God had revealed his will to each of them. Those who had already heard from God simply reinforced what they had said a week earlier, and those who hadn't heard now had a story to tell. Each one had invested his time and heart into his responsibility as an elder of our church. God spoke to one through a passage of Scripture, to another by his father's wisdom, and to another in the middle of the night as he prayed. Each one was convinced that God was leading. We were now of one mind and one heart.

BROADENING THE FOUNDATION

I went to the next tier of leaders in our church, and I told them the story of how God had led us. In public messages and private conversations, members of our board told their own sto ries of God's leading. These stories communicated the unity and power of God's direction and created excitement among our people. Enthusiasm for the vision spread like wildfire. We didn't stop with our board, though. I asked every leader in our church to ask God to confirm his leading, and I gave them a template for their pursuit: PLOW—pray, listen, obey, and God will send us the wow factor of answered prayer. The Scriptures tell us that in a particular village, Jesus "did not do many miracles ... because of their lack of faith" (Matt. 13:58). But as we actively pray for God to lead and change lives, as we listen to his guidance, and as we take bold steps of obedience, he promises to do things we simply can't do. When we see his Spirit doing the impossible, we can only say, "Wow!"

Throughout the body of believers at the Oaks Fellowship, men and women went into their prayer closets to hear from God. Some received words from him fairly quickly, but others wrestled with him for a while. I didn't rush anybody. I wanted them to take all the time they needed, and I answered questions when they wondered about our vision, how to hear from God, and what the process might look like as we followed the Spirit's leading. These weeks of prayer transformed our people from scorekeepers to players in God's vision for our church. If they hadn't heard from God, they'd have been tempted to sit back and make note of every time somebody made a mistake, every time we hit a snag, and every time someone disagreed with a decision. Have you known people like this? They're in every church, from the top-level staff to the most recent visitor. They mark down every flaw, error, and obstacle, making sure to assign blame — and guess who gets the lion's share of that? However, when each leader has heard from God, we trust him through thick and thin, and we trust him together. We don't look for someone to blame. Instead we look for ways to support each other, to work through problems creatively, and to find God in the valley as well as on the mountain. It makes a world of difference.

> However, when each leader has heard from God, we trust him through thick and thin, and we trust him together.

WITHOUT QUESTION, SPIRIT-LED

We don't ask for unanimity in our board about every decision, or even for most decisions. Most of the choices we make aren't as monumental as discerning God's direction to enter chaos at point A and shake up our world! But whether the decisions we face are minor or monumental, we are radically and completely committed to being led by God's Spirit. Seeking direction from God is not optional for us. It's an organizational ethic that's woven deep into the fabric of our church's life.

Nowadays you can find dozens of books about church growth, and many of them have wonderful advice on growing a church. Some of them, however, are primarily based on business principles ... with a little bit of God thrown in for spice. When a church operates solely on business principles, it is relying on the gifting of the pastor, the strength of its marketing, and the willingness of its people to support an inspiring leader's decisions. Strong people on the leadership team may disagree about decisions, and in many cases they will lobby to win support for their side. The business model may be slick and very effective at times, but as a long-term model for church leadership and growth, it's unhealthy. Certainly, we can learn valuable lessons by looking at the way a business organization is operated and led, but ultimately we need to remember that Christ is the head of the universal church and of every local body of believers. The church doesn't exist to make a pastor's plans a reality; it exists to live out Christ's vision for his body and for our community. We don't rely on the brilliance of an individual. We recognize our own faults and failings, as well as our tendency to want acclaim and power. And we trust that God will give us thankful, humble hearts as we get on our knees and hear from him how we should lead his people.

During this time of transition in our church, we redefined the nature of our elder board so it could be more Spirit-led.

> The church doesn't exist to make a pastor's plans a reality; it exists to live out Christ's vision for his body and for our community.

Before, we had been a group of scorekeepers who primarily focused on the budget, the numbers attending in worship, and every other measurable thing in the life of the church. But this crucial juncture led to a dramatic shift in the way we operated. We looked at ourselves and our functions, and we concluded that above all else our primary responsibility was to hear from God and provide leadership in pursuing him. In our meetings, we began talking far more about the Spirit, how to hear God, and the direction he was leading us. Spreadsheets took a backseat.

We changed the agenda of our board meetings. We moved the information, discussion, and action items to the end. To begin each meeting, we spent time worshiping God, focusing on his greatness and goodness, and marveling at his grace and his glory. We didn't just offer a quick prayer and then start looking at budgets. We genuinely worshiped God, and if pouring out our hearts to God took half of our time, it was time well spent. But we didn't move directly into business items after worship. We talked about God's vision and his leading. For several months I asked the elders a series of questions: "What are we most passionate about?" "How do we see God at work among us most powerfully and obviously?" "What needs in our community are we positioned to meet so that we can build bridges with unbelievers?" We thought hard and long about our passions, our giftings, and the needs of our community. As the *leaders* of the church, we realized that our job was to focus our meetings on the most important *priorities* of the church. After that, we often spent time in silent prayer, asking God to speak to each of us about the vision we had discussed. Board members found corners of the room for forty-five minutes or so, and when they came back, I asked them to share what and how God had spoken to them. It was electric! After all the worship, vision casting, and prayer, we carved out time at the end for information, discussion, and action on the budget and schedule. The shift in emphasis changed the culture of our church's top leadership.

Let's be painfully honest for a moment. Leading others can give us a big head sometimes. It feels good when people look up to us and think we're wise and powerful. That was the flaw of the Pharisees; they lived for the acclaim of people. We too can easily get swept up in our prestige as leaders and forget that we are, first and foremost, servants of God and of his people. We lead and serve at *God's* pleasure, not because we've earned it or because we're smarter or more gifted than anyone else. Even our gifts and talents are given to us by God to use for his honor. When church leaders put too much emphasis on business principles, they play the authority and popularity game, trying to win people to their side whenever there is a power struggle or disagreement. Instead, as responsible stewards of God's gifts and mercies, we should look to Christ as our head. We aren't interested in taking sides in an argument; we're interested in seeking God together as we look to him for leadership. We love him with all our hearts, and we serve him the best we know how day in and day out, thanking him for the unspeakable privilege he's given us in his willingness to use us — even us — to touch people's lives.

Let's learn all that we can from business principles but make it a priority to look to the Spirit for guidance. Apply sound management techniques and methods but trust God to change lives. Pursue excellence in all that we do, but do it all with humility and love.

Changes and transitions offer some wonderful opportunities to reemphasize the character of authentic spiritual leadership, but remember that these changes will shake some people to the core. The vast majority of your leaders need some time to adjust to these new realities. When expectations are changed, people have to adjust to new roles, assimilate new responsibilities, and buy into the new vision. Or they need to leave. It's not a tragedy for a few people on a leadership team to say, "I appreciate where you're going, but I don't believe I can go there with you." Some people feel completely comfortable as scorekeepers of budgets and schedules, but they can't make the shift to real spiritual leadership. I've known pastors who implemented this kind of change among their deacons, elders, or governing board, and in many cases a few people concluded they no longer belonged on that team. When this happens, wise shepherds affirm the roles those people have played, and they honor them publicly and privately. They help these men and women find roles that fit their administrative bent, and they celebrate their contribution to the body.

Create a Spirit-led culture so that the pool of candidates for leadership grows in maturity and depth every year. Teach ministry skills and knowledge of the Scriptures, and provide plenty of opportunities for people to serve in leadership throughout the church. Some will rise to the surface and demonstrate exceptional wisdom, discernment, passion, vision, and the ability to influence others. From that rich pool of people, God can show you individuals he's selected to serve with you on your board or in staff positions.

> Create a Spirit-led culture so that the pool of candidates for leadership grows in maturity and depth every year.

CASCADING PRAYER

Earlier we looked at the benefits of cascading communication about the church's vision. The commitment to trust God also cascades from one tier to another until it reaches every person in the congregation. For months our staff prayed together and asked God to clarify his leading. It appeared that he was leading us into chaos, but we weren't willing to impose that decision on anyone. At that point I went to our board and began talking with them about God's direction. We spent months discussing the possibilities and praying before I asked them to trust God for a yes or no.

When we cascaded the vision for the future to the top donors, the lay leaders of the church (teachers, small group leaders, and department heads), all the volunteers, and then the congregation, we asked each group to pray and ask God for clarity and confirmation. We asked people from each group to share with the next tier how God had spoken to them. Vision and prayer go hand in hand.

TIME TOGETHER

We didn't just pray for direction, hear from God, and then close down our prayer lives. Throughout the last several years, we've invested in seasons of corporate prayer so that we could hear from God and trust him together. I first saw the beauty and experienced the power of this kind of prayer because of my father. Years ago he invited everyone in the church to come every Friday night to worship, open our hearts to God, listen, and share with one another what we had heard him say to us. Week after week God showed up to touch people's lives, impart compassion for the lost, and instill in us a vision for reaching even more people. The magnificent thing about this kind of prayer is that God speaks the same thing to many hearts, and when we share with one another, people say, "That's what he told me too," "I sense the same thing," and "He reminded me of the same passage and told me to trust him for great things." When we invite the Spirit to work this way, nobody feels pushed by the pastor to take on responsibilities they didn't want. But we all feel that God is inviting us to join him in a great work.

At the Oaks Fellowship, we've had several seasons of corporate prayer, and even as I write this, we're in the midst of one. Every Tuesday morning at 9:00, we close all our offices and meet for prayer together. Everyone in the church is invited. All of our staff members come, and many of our lay ministry leaders carve out time to join us. People from the congregation, from stay-at-home moms to businesspeople who leave work for an hour, come to be with us. Several business executives bring their staff to pray for our church and to ask God to bless their businesses.

Different staff members lead this time of prayer, and we welcome their passion and creativity. A few weeks ago I led the meeting, and as we prayed, I felt impressed that God wanted to speak to us. Jesus' words in Matthew 4 came to mind: "Man does not live on bread alone, but on every word that comes from the mouth of God." I asked people to open their hearts to God for him to impress on them a passage of Scripture that he would use to guide our church. "The verse God gives you isn't just for you," I told them. "It's his word for our church." I asked them to open their Bibles and wait for the Spirit to lead them. Then, on a big marker board in the front of the room, I asked them to write down the Scripture reference God gave them so we could all look them up and read them. We each sat alone with our Bibles for a while. Slowly at first and then in a rush, about thirty people came up to write on the board. When they finished, the messages formed a cohesive narrative of encouragement and guidance:

> Trust in me.
> I'll show you where to go.
> I will provide for you.
> I'll lead you every step of the way.
> Do not fear when others come against you.
> I'll empower you.
> I will accomplish all that concerns you.

The unity and power of these messages inspired those of us who were there. We wanted to share them with the whole church, so we wrote them down and sent them out to everybody in the church through email. The powerful message that morning came from God through the body of men and women who gathered to trust him together. It didn't come from one person telling them what God said. Instead it came as God spoke to individual hearts and we shared with one another.

Too often we avoid corporate prayer when we need it most: in times of tension and turmoil. Several years ago we went through one of the most difficult transitions in our church's history. We had grown a lot, and we had added many gifted people to our staff team. When I began on staff, it was four or five of my buddies meeting in my office, but we now had fourteen senior staff members. Meeting with each of them every week was absorbing a lot of my time, and none of them felt that they were getting enough attention from me. I tried scheduling more and more time with each of them, but I quickly realized that there simply weren't enough hours in the day! Gradually I realized we would have to change the structure of our staff so that only three or four people reported directly to me, and everybody else reported to them. When the possibility of this shift became known on staff, those who wouldn't be in the top tier felt upset. It was a stressful moment in the life of our church.

> Too often we avoid corporate prayer when we need it most: in times of tension and turmoil.

When couples, friends, or teams experience tension, one of the most common responses is *avoidance*: we back away and avoid the topic that is causing the friction. But that response can be deadly. Instead of avoiding the tension within our staff, I spoke the truth to them and called on them to pray together. I said, "We aren't in alignment, so we need to pray. We're going to meet every day at nine o'clock in the morning to ask God to lead each of us individually and our team corporately."

On the fourth day, God directed me to say something to our staff. I gathered them together during our time of prayer, and I said, "Some of you have said we're in 'a dry place, a desert.' And some of you have said, 'We've lost the joy of serving God.'" I reminded them that at the moment Jesus was baptized, the Father had said, "This is my beloved Son, in whom I am well pleased." The people there that day marveled when they heard the voice speak. In the same way, people in our church had marveled at the outpouring of God's Spirit as we saw him save lost people, restore broken marriages, rescue addicts, give meaning to thousands, and turn darkness into light for countless men and women, young and old. But then, immediately after Jesus' baptism, the Spirit led him into the desert to be tempted and tested. I told our staff, "That's where we are today—we're in the desert to be tested by God and tempted by the Devil. When Jesus came out of the desert, he was full of the Spirit's power, and I believe that will happen to us as well. When we come out of this time of testing, God is going to use us more than ever before. Right now God is preparing us, but soon we'll come out of this time with the Holy Spirit's power."

With that assurance, resistance began to melt, and we were able to trust God more with the future of the church. We didn't try to argue our way out of the relational tension, and we didn't bury our heads and hope it would go away. We held out our hopes and hurts to God and said, "Lord, I'm yours, and we're yours. Do with us what you will, but show us what you want so clearly that we can't miss it." And he did.

Max DePree has said that a leader's primary task is to define reality for his people. That day, God led me to define reality for our staff, putting the events and emotions they were experiencing in the context of God's truth, so we could each respond with faith, hope, and love instead of doubt and fear.

REAL ISSUES, REAL PRAYER

Bold visions drive us to our knees to ask the God of all grace to "rend the heavens and come down" to work among us. When God has led your church to borrow eighteen million dollars when you haven't paid off the previous building yet, it's time to ask him for help. When you are a month away from opening your new building, you have 325 volunteers, and you need 175 more, you plead with God to touch people's lives with a desire to serve. When staff members feel pushed aside and forgotten in the midst of transition, you ask God to give you wisdom to address the problem in a way that honors and encourages those who feel bypassed. When you realize that adding 500 more adults means you'll be adding 125 more kids to your children's ministry, it's time to ask God for wisdom and help. In the early days of planning, these may have been only projections and numbers on a spreadsheet, but as plans became reality, we realized that these were flesh-and-blood people with needs, hopes, and desires.

We also face another dynamic as we lead. When we pursue God to hear his voice, we deal with physical stress and relational tension, but we also experience spiritual conflict—the enemy of our souls wants to get us off track any way he can. We don't need to look for demons behind every bush. There's enough obvious evidence of Satan's work to convince us that the battle is very real. He works in many ways, but most often through distraction, temptation, and accusation.

Author Richard Foster wrote, "Our Adversary majors in three things: noise, hurry and crowds. If he can keep us engaged in 'muchness' and 'manyness,' he will rest satisfied." Satan distracts us by getting our eyes off the ball and onto things that seem more important than they really are. When we pray, seemingly random thoughts enter our heads, and we find ourselves thinking about golf or sex or paying the bills or nursing an insult instead of the issue we began to pray about. Or instead of having a strong attitude of faith as we pray, we may find ourselves thinking of all the reasons why "it can't possibly work." As we work, we are interrupted by "urgent" calls from friends and family, so we fall behind on the things that God has called us to do. It takes discernment to distinguish between distractions and genuine needs, but if the pattern of your thoughts, prayer, and work is frequently interrupted, it may be more than attention deficit disorder.

Since the Garden, Satan has tempted believers to pursue attractive but destructive behaviors. The vast majority of church leaders may steadfastly refuse to give in to overt sexual temptations, but many dabble with pornography. Even more are tempted to excesses in eating and watching television and to harbor a bitter spirit—constantly complaining that they aren't getting what they "deserve." We live in a world of advertising, and each ad is designed to awaken discontent, making us vulnerable to all kinds of temptations. Be aware of your thoughts. Arrest those that wander off, following desires for things that are outside of God's calling, and deal with them ruthlessly.

In churches that have a bold vision—ones that enter the world of chaos—accusations that people make can cause some of the most painful wounds. Because we trust that God wants to use us to do great things, some people will accuse us of arrogance. Change threatens people, and some will react with anger, saying that we don't care about them, that we're building our own kingdoms, and that we're just using them. Accusations that come from outside the camp hurt, but those that come from people we trust hurt far worse.

Don't be deceived. The spiritual battle you face is very real, and even those who pursue God with all their hearts are vulnerable to distractions, temptations, and accusations. Take care of your body, mind, and soul. Get enough rest and exercise. Physical fitness provides stamina and prevents exhaustion that can open doors to spiritual problems. Guard your mind. From time to time, analyze your thought patterns and rivet your mind on the truth of God's Word, his sovereignty and goodness. And feed your soul with the encouragement of trusted friends, input from a mentor, and meaningful times with your family. As Paul told the Ephesians, "Put on the full armor of God so that you can take your stand against the devil's schemes. For our struggle is not against flesh and blood, but against the rulers, against the authorities, against

LEAD *FROM* THE BLESSING
Chris Seidman
The Branch: Farmers Branch, Texas

I've had no shortage of excitement during my last several years in church leadership. There was the challenge of helping a 105-year-old church evolve from a traditional paradigm of worship to a more contemporary approach — and navigating those waters without blowing too big of a hole in the boat; there was the challenge of evolving from a church in one location into a multisite church; there was the time when we laid off several staff members at once due to a financial crunch shortly after expanding to two campuses; oh, and then there were seven

continued on next page…

different occasions when we had to release staff members for matters related to morality or integrity, and a few of those very high-profile staff members.

But my greatest challenge as a leader may not have had as much to do with what was going on around me in any one of those circumstances as it had to do with what was going on within me. The praise of others has long been my elixir of choice. I'm not one of those leaders who can say with relative ease, "I don't really care what they think." I always have cared — sometimes too much and for the wrong reasons.

When a primary leader in an organization is *consumed* with what people may be thinking about him, it can ensnare him and, consequently, the system he is leading in transition moments. There were times when I found myself in a fog of double-mindedness when it came to discerning the right thing to do. Often this was because I was preoccupied with my fear of what others would think about the course of action I was considering. My eyes were focused on the wrong target.

I believe we were all created with a hunger for a sense of worth, significance, and meaning. It's worth noting that the very first thing God did with Adam and Eve after he created them was to "bless" them (Gen. 1:28). The Hebrew word used in that passage carries with it the connotation of verbally bowing one's knee in adoration. God blesses them before he ever gives them a command. He acknowledges them as significant and meaningful before they ever *do* anything. Perhaps this has something to do with us being referred to as human *beings* and not human *doings*.

It's also worth noting that God blesses Jesus in the same way at his baptism. "This is my beloved Son, with whom I am well-pleased" (Matt. 3:17). God's proclamation over Jesus occurred *before* he ever preached to the masses or performed a miracle. Jesus' sense of identity was firmly established in the wake of this blessing. One of the most remarkable things about the leadership of Jesus is that he led *from* the blessing. Most people today lead *for* the blessing. This is where much of the trouble in leadership begins.

I find that when my sense of significance and worth is rooted in what God has proclaimed over me in Christ, I'm truly empowered to lead effectively. With my sense of identity secure, I'm liberated from a preoccupation with what others think of me or how they'll respond. Instead I'm enabled to be completely given over to the integrity of the process of discerning what God is calling us to do. When we lead *from* the blessing instead of *for* the blessing, we're free to lead clearly and uninhibitedly in times of transition. And as goes the leader, so goes the church.

the powers of this dark world and against the spiritual forces of evil in the heavenly realms. Therefore put on the full armor of God, so that when the day of evil comes, you may be able to stand your ground, and after you have done everything, to stand" (Eph. 6:11–13).

A PATTERN FOR CORPORATE PRAYER

For two millennia believers have used the Lord's Prayer to guide them in their pursuit of God. One of the tools we use in our times of corporate prayer is an elaboration of this prayer. We give each person a handout, and we use it as a guide to fix our hearts on God's character and his purposes for us. The handout looks like this:

THE LORD'S
PRAYER GUIDE

Matthew 6:9-13

Introduction: "Teach us to pray"
- Matt. 6:9 "Pray after this manner."
- Luke 11:2 "When you pray, say..."

OUR FATHER WHICH ART IN HEAVEN

- "Father," He is the creative source of us and all things.
- "Our Father," we belong to a family of like persons created in His image.
- "Which art," God exist in the historic past, and is present, today, in the here and now.
- God is "in heaven," a perfect place positioned above all powers and principalities.

HALLOWED BE THY NAME

- Jehovah Jireh (Gen 22:13,14) the Lord will provide (El Shaddai) The all sufficient one
- Jehovah Rapha (Exodus 15:26) the Lord that heals (Elohim) Strong One
- Jehovah Nissi (Exodus 17:15) the Lord our banner (Jehovah Sabaoth) Lord of Host
- Jehovah Shalom (Judges 6:24) the Lord our peace (El Elyon) Most High God
- Jehovah Ra-ah (Psalm 23:1) the Lord is my shepherd (Adonai) Lord
- Jehovah Tsidkenu (Jeremiah 23:6) the Lord our righteousness (M'Kaddesh) Lord My Sanctifier
- Jehovah Shammah (Ezekiel 48:35) the Lord is present (El Olam) The Everlasting God

THY KINGDOM COME, THY WILL BE DONE ON EARTH AS IT IS IN HEAVEN

- God's kingdom come to me, to each member of my family, to my friends, to our church and to our community.
- Pray for God's will to be done in every area of your life. Call the names of persons for whom you're praying, and for those who are in authority. (Pastor, Mayor, governor, Congress, President. 1 Timothy 2:1,2)
- Praise God for His kingdom, power and glory manifested in our world.

GIVE US THIS DAY OUR DAILY BREAD
(Deut. 8:18; Gen 12:2–3; Deut. 28:1–13)

- Pray specifically for God's daily provision for your family. (Philippians 4:19)
- Pray specifically for others who are on your prayer list for financial needs.
- Pray specifically for provision for you church, and other ministries.
- Praise God for His promised and demonstrated provision of daily bread.

FORGIVE US OUR TRESPASSES AS WE FORGIVE THOSE WHO TRESPASS AGAINST US
(Matt 6:14,15; John 20:23)

- Release anyone who has wronged you by vocalizing forgiveness in God's presence.
- Search your heart to confess any sin in your life, and receive His restorative forgiveness. (Psalm 51)
- Praise God for forgiveness of sin and unhindered fellowship in Him. (Psalm 32)

LEAD US NOT INTO TEMPTATION; BUT DELIVER US FROM EVIL

- Pray that the Lord leads you through the day so you can avoid all the traps of temptation that Satan has laid for you. (Matt 26:41; 1 Cor 10:13)
- Claim God's deliverance from the "evil one." Rebuke the evil powers of the North, South, East, and West. Release spiritual prisoners. Pray for the harvest. (Matt 9:38; Luke 10:2) Pray in the ones delivered. (Isaiah 43:1–7; Psalm 107:1–9) Rejoice in the Heavens being opened. (Luke 3:21–22)
- Put on the Christian Soldier's armor (Ephesians 6:11–19), to be prepared for the continuous prayer watch (vs 18–19)

  - Girdle (belt) of truth
  - Breastplate of righteousness
  - Shoes of preparation of the gospel of peace
  - Shield of faith
  - Helmet of Salvation (1 Cor 2:16; Rom 12:2)
  - Sword of the Spirit (Heb 4:12)

- Praise God for guiding your steps so as to avoid the snares of the evil one. (Psalm 37:23)

FOR THINE IS THE KINGDOM, AND THE POWER, AND THE GLORY FOREVER. AMEN

- Begin in praise, continue in praise, and conclude in praise.
- "So be it!"

CONCLUSION:
After exploring His nature in prayer, we find answers for our nature. We are the mirror image of Him! (Gen 1:27)

The leader of the prayer meeting guides the group as we pray through each part of the prayer. We take it slowly, dwelling on each clause and each section, expanding the prayer to include things like the names of God. Working through the prayer like this deepens our understanding of God's character. The leader listens to God during the meeting to creatively guide and direct the focus of our prayers. The phrases of the Lord's Prayer aren't just ritualistic words; when our hearts are engaged in seeking God, the prayer opens us up to his Spirit. For example, at one point the prayer invites us to be honest about our own sins, because we ask God to "forgive our trespasses as we forgive those who trespass against us." These aren't just meaningless words. Together we explore each segment of the prayer, reflecting on the majesty of God, his provision for our needs, his forgiveness of our sins, and his leading and purpose for our future. Not long ago one of our leaders came up to me after our time of prayer and told me, "Pastor, I was a little troubled when I began praying tonight. There's a guy who is upset because of all the changes going on in the church. His feelings are hurt. I was going to ask you to set up a meeting with him, but now I realize that God wants me to talk to him. So Pastor, don't worry about it—I've got it." Notice what God did in this man's heart while we were praying: as we pursued God together, the Lord called him to make a deeper commitment to the transition by taking responsibility for a confused, hurting person.

Corporate prayer isn't just something we do because we're *supposed* to do it. We pray together because God works wonders as his children seek him with one heart and one mind. We don't schedule prayer just when it's convenient. We make it a priority and carve out time that is free from distractions, time when we can fervently ask God to reveal himself. Business principles and practices can help us in the administration of our churches, but we'll never be the people God wants us to be without the transforming truth and power of God.

I've seen God do amazing things in corporate prayer. I've seen people open up their wallets and pocketbooks to pull out hundred-dollar bills, and invite others to give as well, because God told them someone in the room needed help buying groceries that day. I've seen a woman healed of a cancerous spot on her arm—a healing later confirmed by her doctor—and her backsliding husband stand in awe as he saw it happen with his own eyes. I've seen a man healed of cancer in a Wednesday night prayer meeting when he hadn't even been saved yet. I was there when a lady dying of cancer came to a prayer meeting to humbly ask God to touch her "if he wanted to," and he healed her. I've been in prayer meetings where the presence of God was so strong that everyone in the room knew that God was with us and leading us. I've seen hardened hearts melt when God's love touched them, and I've seen God give courage to those who had been timid and fearful.

God will do amazing things when his people make themselves available to him and ask his Spirit to flow through them.

God does marvelous things when his children join together to ask him for help. The prophet Hanani reminded King Asa, "The eyes of the LORD range throughout the earth to strengthen those whose hearts are fully committed to him" (2 Chron. 16:9). God is still looking for people who are willing to commit themselves to him wholeheartedly so he can bless them, use them, and change the world through them. Corporate prayer is an invitation for God to have his way in our hearts and in our church. God will do amazing things when his people make themselves available to him and ask his Spirit to flow through them.

MAPPING YOUR DIRECTION

1. Describe the correlation between bold visions and fervent corporate prayer. How can you keep prayer from being perfunctory?

2. What does it mean for a church to be Spirit-led? How can you tell if leaders are truly trusting God's Spirit to lead them, or if they're just using spiritual words to impress others?

3. Have you ever used the pattern of pursuing God that we used with our board, asking each person to hear from God and come back to report what he said and how he said it? If you have, what were the benefits? If not, is this something you want to do? Why or why not?

4. What are some evidences of spiritual conflict you've experienced in times of transition, specifically distractions, temptations, and accusations? Did you recognize them at the time? If so, how did you respond? If not, what helped you recognize them later?

5. What insights or processes in this chapter were most helpful to you? Explain your answer.

6. What are some steps you want to take with your staff, board, lay leaders, and congregation regarding corporate prayer and trusting God together?

CHAPTER 6

RECOGNIZING OPPORTUNITIES AND AVOIDING OBSTACLES

The harder the conflict, the more glorious the triumph. What we obtain too cheap, we esteem too lightly; it is dearness only that gives everything its value. — THOMAS PAINE, AMERICAN REVOLUTIONARY, RADICAL, AUTHOR OF *COMMON SENSE*

Outstanding leaders have the ability, often with the help of a wise friend or mentor, to take full advantage of opportunities and turn obstacles into stepping stones of progress. They learn to see every situation through the lens of faith. Times of transition and chaos create new opportunities and lead to unforeseen difficulties. If we don't anticipate these new realities and take advantage of them, we'll fail to respond in a way that builds trust with our people and advances the kingdom. In this chapter, I want to offer a few principles and practical tips about seizing opportunities and overcoming obstacles.

OPPORTUNITIES COME KNOCKING

All leaders lead, but gifted leaders in any field have the ability to see open doors where others only see walls. One of the most important principles of spiritual leadership, one that is woven throughout this book, is that we need to constantly open our hearts to God, ask him for direction, and watch for signs of his leading. With a spirit of anticipation, we won't get bogged down in business as usual. Instead we'll have what Bill Hybels calls "holy discontent," and like the cartoon character Popeye, we'll look at the people around us, our hearts will break for those who suffer and wander, and we'll say, "That's all I can stand. I can't stand no more!"

I've been around people with this spirit of anticipation, and I've been infected with their disease. They're always looking for the next open door, and they're not afraid of the hard work, diligent prayer, and personal sharpening it takes to walk through those doors. No matter how many people they touch, they are aware that there are still countless others who need the grace of God. As in the parable of the wedding banquet, they know that there is still room for more at the feast of God's kingdom celebration.

Love for Christ drives us to find new opportunities to reach lost people. That's the reason we take bold steps at point A and enter chaos. That's the reason our church is expanding with a multisite strategy to reach people in other communities. That's the reason we are dedicated to leadership development so that we have godly, skilled men and women to lead the full spectrum of ministries at every location. And that's the reason we form partnerships with outstanding organizations so that we leverage our resources for greater impact.

> Success is the place where preparation, courage, and opportunity meet.

Success is the place where preparation, courage, and opportunity meet. Years ago a good friend of mine was speaking at a conference of eight thousand students. On the third night of the event, he came to me a few minutes before he was to speak and said, "Scott, I believe the Lord wants you to speak tonight."

I'm not sure what look I had on my face, but all I could think to say was, "You've got to be kidding!"

"No," he said, smiling. "I'm going to say a few words about the negative perception most adults have of young people today, and then I want you to come up and take the microphone out of my hand and start preaching. God has something to say through you tonight."

He didn't ask me if I wanted to preach, and he didn't tell me what to say. He just said, "Hey, you're on in a few minutes. Bring it!"

I hadn't even brought my Bible to the conference, and I certainly hadn't prepared a talk. Going behind the curtain, I got on my knees and said, "Lord, I'm yours, and these kids are yours. If you want me to speak, you've got to give me a message." He reminded me that he had been preparing me for this moment for the last several years, and he gave me confidence that he would speak through me.

My friend began his message as I waited off stage. He told the audience that they had been labeled an aimless generation, a generation that didn't care about anything but themselves, but God hadn't counted them out. That was my cue. I walked onto the stage to take the mic from him. But there was a slight problem: he had forgotten to tell the security guards that I was going to speak, so two big dudes grabbed me by each arm to yank me off the stage! My friend quickly intervened and assured them he wanted me to speak. Thankfully, they released me. I turned and looked at eight thousand eager kids who desperately needed to hear an encouraging word from the Lord. Praying a quick, silent prayer for help, I opened my mouth and told them, "This is a generation that God has his hand on. This is a generation that says, 'Here I am, God. I'm all yours.' You're saying, 'God, if you want to feed people, I want to be bread in your hands. If you want to fight for justice, I'll be a sword in your hands. God, if you want to build your kingdom, I want to be a hammer you can use. And if for some crazy reason you want to throw a tea party, then I'm a little teapot short and stout, here is my handle, here is my spout. When I get all steamed up, you're gonna hear me shout: "Just tip me over, and *pour me out!*"'" Those students went crazy. Somehow the combination of powerful metaphors, blended with their childhood memories of the teapot song, captured their hearts that night, and God worked in wonderful ways.

The next day people came up to me and said, "Man, you are so lucky to get the opportunity to speak like that." But I don't think it was luck at all. All of my Bible study and speaking during the previous few years had prepared me, and God picked that moment to use me. I could have said no to my friend, but I felt

RISKS AND REWARDS
John Bishop
Living Hope Church: Vancouver, Washington

I love the local church. I love fast-paced environments. I love new challenges. Most of all, I love to see lives transformed. I love being part of a team that dreams together and sees the impossible become reality.

When that happens, we know it's something *only God* could have done.

The day we decided to open five multisite campuses on the same day has become one of the most blessed — yet difficult — times of transition in the history of our church. On that day, more than just our ministry changed; the entire culture of our church changed. The idea of launching multiple locations at the same time began with a simple thought: "If Starbucks can do it, why can't the church do it?" After all, why should coffee get all the good press? The church has to be risking more than a coffee shop does.

Still, when you risk, you *will* fail. If you aren't failing at something right now, you are not risking enough. We found there were many blessings that resulted from that decision. We found we had more people serving, we were growing in momentum, and lots of people were coming to Christ. But along with the blessings, there were multilayered challenges: structural issues, communication issues, leadership issues, and quality control issues. We eventually worked through all of these challenges, but they weren't easy.

> If you aren't failing at something right now, you are not risking enough.

Steering through times of chaos in the midst of transition has been difficult for our church — to say the least! Since we are located in one of the most unchurched parts of the United States, we have had to be willing to do *whatever* it takes to reach that one person for Christ. The costs have been high, but we think they've been worth it.

"Risk to reach and reach to release" has now become the DNA of Living Hope Church. In just five years we have grown in weekend attendance from 450 people to well over 5,000; most of those are first-time believers. The pain has been worth the cost. By God's grace, we have seen over 4,000 people baptized at Living Hope in just the last thirty-six months. Our story is one of ongoing transitions, changing structures, and constant attempts at adapting to chaotic circumstances.

that I would be saying no to God. There was a sizeable knot of fear in my stomach when I walked onstage that night, but I chose to trust God.

Opportunities come in all shapes and sizes. Some occur spontaneously, like being asked to speak on the spot, while others take place through the seasonal flow of events in the life of a church. Still others happen during times of transition. Let's examine a few of the opportunities that come through the various seasons and circumstances of ministry.

Seasonal Momentum

It amazes me that some pastors and staff fail to capitalize on the natural momentum of the church calendar. The principle is simple: if you connect spiritual momentum with seasonal momentum, you'll have massive momentum. It's not rocket science. In Dallas, Texas, there are two key points in the year for launching new programs and encouraging a renewed focus on evangelism: when school starts in the fall, and at the start of the New Year, in early January. We find that the energy, expectancy, and enthusiasm of our congregation tend to peak at these two times. That energy will often continue through the fall until Thanksgiving, and then again in the winter and spring until Easter. But from Thanksgiving through the end of the year, we find we're in a lull. People are often busy and distracted with various family and holiday activities. Of course, we emphasize the Christmas celebration, but that's the only spike in attendance during this downtime. Similarly, we find that after Easter, families are preparing for graduation, weddings, and all kinds of other events at the end of the school year. Throughout the summer they are preoccupied until school starts again.

> The principle is simple: if you connect spiritual momentum with seasonal momentum, you'll have massive momentum.

That's not to say that we shut down our programs and go into hibernation during these lulls. Our pastoral staff and lay leadership use these times as preparation for launching new initiatives when the cycles pick up in September and January. We teach classes on relational evangelism, work on videos, and recruit and train volunteers in anticipation of additional growth during the next cycle of high momentum. It may look as if there's not as much going on during slower times in the seasonal cycle, but we're not just sitting around taking it easy. We're focused, committed, and active in our preparation so that we can capture as much momentum as possible in the next up-cycle.

We schedule evangelistic outreaches during the natural-momentum times of the year in the fall and the winter and early spring. During these times, our people are more focused and energized, and their friends are more willing to come to church, because they aren't as distracted.

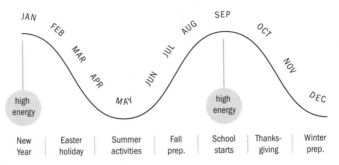

In some parts of the rural Midwest, harvest season is a short but crucial time of the year. Schools close, and everybody helps bring in the crops. The livelihood of the entire community depends on those few weeks. In the same way, the harvesttimes in our church are in the fall after school starts and in the winter after New Year's. During these times, we need everyone focused on reaching the lost. And during the downtimes, we focus our efforts on building barns (small groups) and getting our systems ready to handle the next harvest.

When you move to a new area, ask questions to learn any idiosyncrasies of the community, and make adjustments to adapt to the culture of that area. Most communities follow time-tested patterns. The cycle for our church has both times of preparation and times of capturing momentum. All of our yearly planning centers around this cycle, and it consistently produces results.

New Creativity

Many people today, especially those in the younger generation, are surrounded by new media technology and operate in environments of high visual and audio stimulation. While some church leaders resent the fact that our culture is highly visual and entertainment-oriented, we can't ignore these changing realities. If we insist on doing church the way our grandparents did it, these young people will simply go somewhere else. Let me clarify what I'm saying so you don't misunderstand me. I'm not suggesting that we shift our focus and begin entertaining people instead of teaching the Scriptures and calling them to radical commitment to Christ. The call of God has not changed; we are to live with the same devotion to Christ as those who followed him a generation ago—or in the first century. We simply need to be aware of the way that people assimilate concepts today and to eliminate any barriers that keep them from learning and growing in their faith.

> We simply need to be aware of the way that people assimilate concepts today and to eliminate any barriers that keep them from learning and growing in their faith.

Most church leaders have found that people will be far more open to the call of Christ if we present God's truth with a bit of creativity. Our goal isn't to get laughs or wows but to win a hearing for the gospel. In our church, God has given us some incredibly creative people who have a knack for connecting people's hearts with biblical concepts. For example, we've done some teaching series that are introduced by videos each week of me with each of my sons doing some crazy things. One series was called Worst-Case Scenarios. My son Dillon and I went dogsledding in the North Woods of Minnesota in the dead of winter, and the video clips showed how we coped with difficulties. In the message series, I related God's perspective about how we can survive, and even thrive, in hard times. Dakota and I did a series of videos at Universal Studio's Islands of Adventure for a series called Theologgins for Your Noggins, with messages featuring some of the books written by the great theologian Dr. Seuss. A third series features Hunter and me, with another pastor and his son, on a motorcycle road trip across Texas. Both that pastor's church and ours will teach the same series about the process of following Christ, using the metaphor of a father and son traveling down the highway to scenic destinations, kind of like John Bunyan's classic *Pilgrim's Progress*. These series are put together in a fresh, creative way to provide the best opportunity for people in our congregation to invite their non-Christian friends to church to hear the gospel.

New Buildings

In the first few weeks after you open a new worship facility, church-growth experts say, you can expect a 25 to 40 percent increase in attendance. That, my friends, is momentum! But this momentum quickly fades if you haven't prepared the infrastructure necessary to serve all the new people.

Six months before the doors opened on our building, I asked all of our staff and key lay leaders to let me know how many additional volunteers they would need when God brought 25 to 40 percent more people. We couldn't afford to be caught short. We needed to identify, recruit, and train the additional childcare workers, greeters, parking lot attendants, ushers, youth workers, and volunteers in every ministry of the church. With this input, we calculated that we needed five hundred more volunteers. With this information, we launched a campaign called "Unprecedented Opportunities." I told our people that God was giving us an opportunity to touch lives that would never happen again in the life of our church. I reminded them that we couldn't live on our past successes or just hope people would stay with us after the doors opened. We had to be prepared. I explained that we needed five hundred new volunteers to serve wherever they felt God wanted them to serve. We wanted them to be in a place where they could use their God-given gifts and talents, where they'd feel excited to touch lives each week, and where they'd have the greatest sense of fulfillment. I didn't ask them to sign up on that first week of the campaign. I only wanted them to think, pray, and talk to people in the atrium of the church about the opportunities that were available. I invited people to go online and take spiritual gifts assessments and personality tests and view job descriptions for each volunteer role. When they were ready, we asked them to select a place where they felt called to serve. Signing up on that subsequent morning was only the *beginning* of the process. Our leaders contacted each person who signed up, and they held meetings to inform, encourage, and train each of these new recruits.

Opening the doors on a new building is exciting, and it attracts people who have never come to your church before. But the honeymoon phase of a new facility can be short-lived. If you want people to stay, you have to recruit and train skilled, motivated volunteers to serve them.

New Strategies

We've been doing multisite ministry long before multisite was the norm. Our campus in Red Oak is really just an extension of our church in Oak Cliff. Expansion is in our DNA, and we're always looking for opportunities to open new campuses. We've seen God provide these opportunities time after time. At one point, the pastor of a church a few miles away came to see me and offered us his building. He was ready to retire, and he thought we could reach people in his community more effectively than anyone else.

On another occasion, our denomination had an unfinished building near us, but they couldn't find the funds to complete it. They asked if we could use it. We prayed, and God led us to step out in faith to finish the building. We were able to finish the construction on the 66,000-square-foot building in five months. We opened a school there for five hundred elementary-age kids, and we used the third floor for our School of Ministry and Leadership. Just recently we began discussions with Southwestern Assembly of God University in Waxahachie, Texas, my alma mater, to become one of their adjunct campuses. We worked out a partnership with the school in which members of our staff would serve as professors, mentoring students in ministry strategy and skills. This has proved to be the perfect training environment, providing the credibility of a respected university, the funding of generous people, and competent, godly professors to teach and model what it means to walk with God and touch people's lives. Our collaboration with the school is the pipeline of leadership for our multisite strategy. In every case, God presented the opportunity. All we had to do was figure out the details and walk through an open door.

Far too often leaders fail to see opportunities because we're blinded by the urgent, nagging problems right in front of us. Some pastors become so overwhelmed and discouraged by the problems of the people they serve that they aren't able to step back and see the big picture. When this happens, pastors abdicate their role as visionary leaders and focus all their time and attention on solving problems. Sadly, this can happen to any of us.

> Far too often leaders fail to see opportunities because we're blinded by the urgent, nagging problems right in front of us.

Every member of a church's leadership team needs to carve out time to pray, think, and dream so they can clearly identify the opportunities God has given them. We need to balance the need for visionary insight with the reality of urgent, pressing problems. I ask my staff to write ninety-day plans that have two basic elements: the opportunities for them to seize and the problems they need to solve. If they can identify these two elements, they'll have bite-sized goals they can chew on, and most of the time they'll see dramatic progress. Most often you'll find that some people have a natural tendency to be visionary, while some gravitate toward problem solving. Because I ask *all* of my staff to focus on *both* of these issues, each person is able to operate in his or her strength while remaining aware of the need for a balanced perspective. The goals they set in these ninety-day windows are seldom overwhelming, and if they accomplish them, they feel genuine job satisfaction—which builds energy and confidence for the next ninety days. In fact, I'm a firm believer in the football strategy of picking up first downs one after another. If an offense does that long enough, they'll score a touchdown.

Each ministry leader can use the ninety-day plan to focus on first downs that take them a step toward their long-term goal. Their first downs may be getting the right person for an important leadership role, coordinating a plan with other ministries, finding the best transportation for a trip, designing the promotional piece for an outreach, organizing and conducting a planning meeting for an upcoming event, and so on. These may not seem significant in themselves, but the big-splash events won't be successful without success in these preparation steps.

I'm seldom worried or upset if someone tries and fails. I'm only really concerned if I don't see any effort or creativity. People often join our staff or lay leadership teams with a fear of failure or rejection, so they're timid with their plans. I work hard to intentionally define the atmosphere by rewarding boldness and creativity. When staff and lay leaders see me applaud someone who has tried something new and failed miserably, they will realize that failure isn't the end of the world. The seeds of boldness and creativity grow best in the soil of relational security.

Whether our plans succeed or fail, we still take the time to evaluate everything we do. We don't just look at success or failure and shrug our shoulders. Organizations only improve if they analyze what went right, what went wrong, and how they can improve next time. Fearful people dread this moment, so we need to assure them that our analysis isn't meant to condemn them. Some people on your team may need additional reassurance, and in some cases you'll need to tread lightly with the analysis until you've earned their trust. After a while your team members will recognize that the environment is safe and that failure doesn't result in condemnation. We'll be more effective in our ministry when we engage in honest, positive, forward-looking evaluation of every event or program we lead.

Evaluations like this are simply a matter of faithful stewardship. For example, there are thousands of wonderful ministries that we can support with our financial resources. Every believer has more requests for funds than he or she has money to give, and every church has countless opportunities to touch lives. While all these ministries may be good and worthwhile, we certainly can't support them all. We need to be selective in our giving, and we utilize a grid that reflects our vision statement and our core values. In a similar way, we need to make sure that we evaluate every opportunity according to our benchmarks, and this evaluation tells us whether or not we should dive in, pass, or tell the person or organization that we may be interested in the future. We can't afford to dilute our influence and drain our energies by trying to do everything. We have to constantly come back to God's calling for our church and invest every dollar, every hour, every room, and every person in the specific things God has given us a green light to do. Some of our staff have big hearts and are so gracious that they want to help every person and ministry that knocks on our doors, but part of my role is to teach them the importance of aligning our activities and resources with our vision and values. I don't need to be harsh in correcting them. After all, their hearts are in the right place, and there's nothing wrong with their motives. But since we can't help everybody, we must remain focused on God's unique calling for our church.

I believe God puts phenomenal opportunities around us. We just need to open our eyes to notice them, align them with the vision he has given us, and then trust him to change lives as we take action.

CREATIVE PROBLEM SOLVING

There are thousands of books that will give you untold ways of solving problems. Most of these problem-solving methods work most effectively in specific fields, such as engineering or manufacturing. But all models of problem solving contain common components: analysis, planning, marshalling resources, communication, implementation, and fine tuning. At our church, we use a planning model called Six Thinking Hats.[11] This simple model has produced profound results for us. Some companies use a very sophisticated approach called Six Sigma,[12] which requires top-level employees to go through certified training before they implement the strategy. In this chapter, I'm not going to take the time to outline a comprehensive strategy for solving problems in your church. Instead I want to offer a few insights about the nuances of fixing problems in church settings, where the spiritual dimension of ministry often leads to unrealistic expectations.

Years ago, when I was a youth pastor, I not only *had* a problem, I *was* the problem. Most youth pastors are far more humble and mature than I was at the time. I thought I had the ins and outs of ministry all figured out, but I was failing miserably in my communication with parents. Quite often parents would come up to me and say things like, "Scott, why can't you tell us the schedule of events a couple of months in advance? You need to be more organized." Or "It would be really helpful if we knew about the schedule for summer camp [or an overnight or an outreach, a trip to Six Flags, or dozens of other events for students] more than a week or two before it begins. We've already planned our vacation. If we'd known, we could have planned differently." Every time a parent had a question or a problem, I branded them chronic complainers.

One day three parents called me to complain, and their calls sent me over the edge. I'd had enough. After the last call, I put the phone down and prayed, "Lord, what's wrong with these people? Don't they understand that I'm working like crazy to lead their kids to Christ and help them grow in their faith? Can't they appreciate all I'm doing for you and for them? To be honest, God, these complaining parents are the ones causing most of the damage in the lives of their kids, damage I'm trying to repair!"

Pouring out my anger to God felt really good at first. Then God spoke to my heart: "Scott, you're the problem, not them. You're not willing to listen to their input and make changes. You're missing the opportunity. They're saying you need help, and what you don't realize is that they're willing to be the ones to help you." I was shocked and embarrassed, but God's words had the ring of truth. In the depths of my heart I knew he was right.

I invited the five most influential parents, the ones who had complained the loudest about my leadership, to come over to our house. Jenni made sure we had cheesecake—because it's hard to be mad when you're eating cheesecake—and we talked for a few minutes before the main event. After people felt comfortable, I picked up a legal pad and a pen and told them, "I'm so glad you came tonight, because I'm in desperate need of your help. I've been praying and thinking about the things you've said to me concerning the changes you'd like to see in the youth ministry. I want you to give me your input about how I can do a better job helping you raise your children to be champions for Christ." Then I poised my pen so everyone could see I was ready to take notes.

The room was as silent as a tomb. The parents were dumb-founded that my resistance to them had flipped 180 degrees and I was now asking for their input. Gradually they began to speak up, and soon I had two pages full of their ideas. When they were finished, I looked at the list and saw that the needs they had identified fell into three categories: planning, communication, and the need for more volunteer leaders. I asked if I was hearing them accurately, and they all said, "Yes, that's it."

I looked at them and said, "Thank you for your input. Now I want to ask you to prayerfully consider becoming my parent sponsors to give me input and feedback so our ministry becomes what God wants it to be. I'd like to meet with you during the year before each season. I'll bring you the plan, the schedule, and the budget so you can let me know if I forgot anything, and I need your help to communicate with the other parents. Will you pray about that role? We'll meet again in a month to get your answer and talk about our plans for the summer."

Four weeks later we met, and they reviewed my plans for an upcoming parents' meeting. When I met with the other parents, the input I had received from my parent sponsors changed every-thing. Instead of having parents get frustrated and ask a lot of questions because I hadn't given them enough details, I was able to give them all the information they needed. After I prayed at the end of the meeting, the entire group of parents stood and cheered! It was amazing. Some of them came up to me after the meeting. They hugged me and said, "Scott, this is the best parents' meeting I've ever attended. It was awesome!" They were astonished at the changes. In the past I had been disorganized, but now I was organized. I had been defensive, but now I was confident and gracious; I had seen parents as the problem, but now I saw them as partners.

Today that small group of parent sponsors has grown into a group of about fifty adult leaders who assist our student ministry team on a regular basis. It's a glorious thing to see, and it all started when God showed me that the people I saw as problems could be the solutions to my struggles. The problem, it turned out, wasn't them — it was me.

We experience problems of all stripes, but they take on far more significance when we make them personal and infuse them with emotion. Then the issues aren't processes and communication; they're personal identity, security, turf, and prestige. Many of us are surprisingly fragile, and when we make procedural difficulties into personal problems, we get hurt by even the smallest disagreements. That's what I had done with the parents' complaints. They just wanted better communication, but I had interpreted their request as a personal condemnation of my life and ministry, so I retaliated by branding them as bad people.

Let me offer a few suggestions that can help take the destructive power out of problems and enable us to find creative, effective solutions.

Normalize the Reality of Problems

I believe there are two errors that spiritual leaders commonly make when they communicate with people: they either wear a mask of perfection and never admit they struggle with anything, or they bare it all and say too much. Both approaches can result in eroded trust with their staff and congregations, but in my observations, the first error is far more common. We all have a natural habit of hiding our flaws from others. So to combat this tendency, from time to time I remind everyone that we all have problems and make mistakes. But we need to balance our authenticity with discretion and wisdom. When I preach, I will sometimes share my own struggles, but I make sure that my authenticity is always coupled with the hope Jesus offers. I don't share my deepest, darkest struggles with the congregation until God has given me wisdom and I've taken a step or two toward the solution. People need to know we're real, but they also need to know that God works through long, slow processes as well as in miraculous ways.

People need to know we're real, but they also need to know that God works through long, slow processes as well as in miraculous ways.

On an organizational level, people on our staff and in our church need to know that I'm aware of problems they face and that I understand what they are feeling. They don't demand that I solve these problems immediately. They just need to see that I'm not clueless and detached from the problems they are confronting. When they know that I understand, they trust that I will work hard to find an answer for them, and they're willing to wait patiently. They may even get involved and become part of the solution.

Watch for Flash Points

When you find yourself responding to problems in an emotionally charged way, try to uncover and examine hidden areas of pain or irritation. Some of us feel threatened when we fail, because we're insecure. We may teach boldly about the grace of God, but the way we respond to failure shows that we still live in fear—and fear is a very powerful motivator. Another common flash point occurs when we grow bitter and resentful as a way of punishing people who, we perceive, have wronged us. When an emotional response (such as anger, fear, or hurt) is out of proportion with the event or circumstance, you can be sure there's something hidden underneath your heart that's fueling those feelings.

If you try to shove down or ignore these painful emotions, they'll just fester and surface again at a later time in even more powerful ways. Instead of ignoring these feelings, we need to open our hearts to the Lord and ask, "Father, what's this about? Help me see the unresolved hurts that are causing me to react in this way." Find a quiet place where you can listen to God as he speaks to your heart. We need to take time, when our hearts are heated or wounded, to let the Lord remind us of hurts or dashed hopes from the past that are coloring our lives today. We need to be honest about the past and trust God to heal these hurts in his way and in his timing. Try talking to a trusted friend to get insight and encouragement, and fix your thoughts on the magnificent truths of God's love, forgiveness, purpose, and power. Deep emotional wounds won't heal instantly, but with the healing power of God's grace and truth, we can choose to respond differently when circumstances open old wounds.

Don't Jump to Conclusions

We are often eager to assume that a difficulty we experience is "that person's problem" or a demonic attack, but we would be wise to consider God's purpose for our struggles. Our difficulties may be the consequence of a natural disaster, the result of a human "accident," a wound inflicted by an evil person, or hurts caused by a person who loves us. Many of our struggles are self-inflicted. Whatever the cause, God wants to use these struggles to test our faith and make us stronger. We can trust him to give us the perception and tenacity we need to respond appropriately. The apostle Paul experienced his share of suffering and rejection, but God graciously gave him insight into his situation, and he was able to respond with trust and hope in God's greater purpose. He wrote, "We also rejoice in our sufferings, because we know that suffering produces perseverance; perseverance, character; and character, hope. And hope does not disappoint us, because God has poured out his love into our hearts by the Holy Spirit, whom he has given us" (Rom. 5:3–5).

When we have the right perspective, we don't deny or minimize the problems in our life. Nor do we blame others and excuse ourselves when we're the ones to blame. The right perspective on our problems will bring us face-to-face with the brutal reality of our failures and our pain while reminding us of the hope-filled presence and purpose of God.

Triage

In an emergency room, the triage nurse determines which patients need immediate care and which can wait for the next available doctor. A good triage nurse is able to discern the problem and decide which issues are truly life threatening. Remember, every problem you face is not the end of the world. Some issues need to be addressed immediately, but others not only *can* wait but *must* wait until you have more information, you have a better process in place, or you sense that God's timing is right.

The triage nurse observes the patient, asks questions, and then assesses the situation carefully. When a problem arises, we should do exactly the same thing. Instead of reacting immediately to every new problem, we can often benefit by taking a little time to notice things, ask questions, and see if we can uncover any aspects that weren't obvious at first glance. Quite often just a few questions can surface factors that completely change our assessment and the solution we choose.

Be Patient

Some people are ready to take action at the drop of a hat, while others painstakingly analyze every detail before they move a muscle. Neither frantic activity nor analysis paralysis is helpful when we need to solve a problem. The bigger the problem, the more we must rely on God's timing for the solution — and the biggest problems are almost always people problems. When you talk with people who are angry or discouraged, don't jump to give them answers right away. Take time to ask more questions and show them that you care about them. Most of the time, people need your love more than they want your quick solutions to their problems.

> The bigger the problem, the more we must rely on God's timing for the solution — and the biggest problems are almost always people problems.

When you ask additional questions, you may find that the real problem is much different than what you first assumed it was. Even then, don't rush in to fix the problem. Most often it's wise to involve the person in the formulation of the answer and the process of resolution. This of course takes additional time, but it trains the person to think, plan, pray, and look to God for his wisdom and timing. And that's crucial—in fact, it's even more important than finding the solution.

Get Outside Input

When I've been confused about a sticky problem, mentors have given me the input I needed. Even when I thought I knew exactly what to do, talking with them sharpened my thinking and shaped my direction. We'll look at this resource in more detail in chapter 8, but for now realize that a leader, even an on-the-edge visionary, doesn't have to walk alone. The family of God isn't a blessing just for new believers—it's for mature leaders as well. Find someone you trust, and ask them for advice.

Moving into a time of transition will multiply your problems. If you want to have a calm, easy life, avoid chaos and run from change as fast as you can! The good news is that our problems don't have to weigh us down. With God's perspective and faithful reliance on his grace, we can thrive in times of stress.

MAPPING YOUR DIRECTION

1. On a scale of zero to ten, how skilled are you at seeing opportunities? Explain your answer. How would your staff rate you? How would your spouse rate you?

2. What are the big opportunities you need to seize as a church in the next ninety days?

3. Draw a chart of the seasonal momentum of your community and your church. How well are you capturing the high-momentum seasons? How well are you preparing during the downtimes in the schedule?

4. How well are you capturing the momentum created by new buildings, new creativity, and new strategies?

5. How would it help you and your staff to identify "first downs" by using ninety-day planning cycles to seize opportunities and fix problems?

6. What are some flash points you've seen in yourself and in leaders around you? When you've seen a flash point in someone else, did you help the person uncover the hidden energy source? How might it help to do that?

7. Describe what triage might look like when problems are brought to you.

8. What specific applications from this chapter will you implement in your own life and in your team?

CHAPTER 7

CELEBRATE EVERY STEP OF THE WAY

Joy is the serious business of Heaven. — C. S. LEWIS

Pastors typically fall into two broad categories. Some are problem solvers. They love to counsel people and help them overcome the difficulties they face in their families and their personal lives. These pastors would normally be very grateful for the good things they see God doing, but in too many cases they are simply exhausted and experience constant "compassion fatigue." Another group of pastors are what I call the "go-for-broke visionaries." They're future focused, always thinking about the next big thing. Often they are so emotionally, spiritually, and physically stretched to accomplish far-off goals that they fail to stop and appreciate the Spirit's work today.

Unfortunately, neither of these groups is very good at celebrating.

Gratitude for what God has done and will do should be a natural and normal part of our life and ministry. The Psalms contain countless admonitions to praise God for every conceivable characteristic and gift, and we need to follow that advice. The overflow of gratitude transforms attitudes, inspires hearts, affirms our calling, and builds relationships. Celebration isn't optional. It's not just for those celebrating a victory—it's a discipline that sustains those who are living in the midst of the battle.

GOOD EXAMPLES

Author and pastor John Piper reminds us that joy is central to the nature of Christ. Everything that Jesus said and did flowed out of his joy in serving the Father. His joy wasn't forced or obligatory; it flowed freely out of a heart aligned with God's perspective and priorities. When the seventy-two disciples returned from their missionary exploits and reported to Jesus, "Lord, even the demons submit to us in your name," Jesus' joy couldn't be contained. He was thrilled at what they had done, and he burst out in spontaneous praise to the Father (Luke 10:1–24).

Jesus carried the weight of the entire world on his shoulders, but nothing could stop him from enjoying every step of faith taken, every insight gained, and every act of service performed by those around him. At the close of his earthly ministry, he instituted the Lord's Supper to remind us to constantly celebrate the wonder of God's love and mercy. These punctuated moments of genuine celebration are a gift from God, an opportunity to stop, reflect, and thank him for his matchless grace.

Another man who exuded joy and celebrated the goodness of God was the apostle Paul, perhaps the second-busiest man the world has ever known. Paul was a missionary, a writer, a teacher, and a tentmaker. He faithfully carried the message of Christ to every corner of the known world, and he cared deeply about people—especially those who had never heard the gospel. Paul could have allowed himself to be consumed by the problems he faced or spent his time worrying about the future. But he chose instead to celebrate the wonder of God's great mercy and love. Celebration—full of praise, gratitude, and encouragement—was a priority for Paul. He reminded the believers in Philippi about the encouragement, comfort, tenderness, and compassion they enjoyed in their relationship with Christ, and then he directed them to let their relationships with each other reflect the love Christ had shown them. Paul wrote that their love for each other would "make my joy complete" (Phil. 2:2). Paul celebrated the good things that God was doing in the lives of others, and was blessed to see others blessed by God.

THE REAL THING

I realize that I've joined a number of emotions and concepts together here. Some people might take issue with lumping joy, celebration, praise, and thanksgiving together. Certainly, there are important differences in the way each of these are expressed, but I would argue that all of these are simply different expressions of biblical worship. Each one is a response to the nature of God, his work in the universe, the beauty of his creation, his incredible grace and truth, and the countless gifts he gives us. I don't think it matters to God how we articulate the distinctions between these words — he just delights to receive our gratitude and praise as it spills out of hearts overflowing with love for him.

One of my favorite stories in the New Testament — and one that challenges me to the core of my being — is Luke's account of the ten lepers who came to Jesus (Luke 17:11 – 19). They cried out to Jesus for help, and he gave them a simple command: show yourselves to the priests. On the way to the priests, the lepers were miraculously healed, but only one of them, a Samaritan, came back, fell at Jesus' feet, and poured out his thanks to him. Every time I think of that event, I ask myself, "Am I more like the thankless nine or the one who came back to give thanks to Jesus?" As a pastor, I get to see God do wonderful things in people's lives day after day. It's easy to grow accustomed to the wonder of what God is doing, and it becomes a routine part of my life. But if I don't stop to thank God (and tell others what he's done), I rob him of the praise he's due, and I rob myself and others of the thrill of connecting with God to thank him for his goodness and grace.

Celebration isn't something pastors can just delegate to others. We can ask others to lead and administrate in many other areas of the church's life, but if we're not taking the lead in giving thanksgiving and praise, people will assume that it's not very important. No matter what our printed vision and values statements say, the things we model become the actual values of the staff team and the entire church.

At its heart, celebration focuses primarily on the work of God in people's lives, but another essential part of celebration is affirming

> No matter what our printed vision and values statements say, the things we model become the actual values of the staff team and the entire church.

one another. We build up and bless each other when we communicate messages of "I love you," "I'm proud of you," "You're terrific at this or that," and "I can see a great future for you." These messages thrill our souls when we hear them, and they build trust and love when we speak them to others. These messages, though, have to be genuine. Sadly, I've known church staff, employees, and children who heard the right words spoken from a wrong heart. The messages were used to manipulate and control, not to affirm and free the hearer to fly higher than ever before.

And sometimes the people who hear these messages are afflicted with false humility, so they can't really receive them. You know the type: we offer sincere appreciation, but the person says, "Oh, it wasn't me. It was the Lord." That comment sounds really spiritual, but it's an unwillingness to accept praise. Why do people respond this way? This reaction to affirmation may have been modeled for them, or maybe they suffer from a deep sense of shame and don't feel worthy of love and praise. In other cases, it may be a deeper issue of hidden pride, the root of false humility.

THE POWER OF CELEBRATION

Dietrich Bonhoeffer was, perhaps, the leading theologian and activist of the twentieth century. No one could doubt the depth of his commitment to Christ. In fact, he wrote one of the most quoted statements of the century: "When Christ calls a man, he bids him come and die." But Bonhoeffer wasn't a stern, sullen, intense man. His jailers in the Nazi concentration camp were impressed with his calm demeanor, steadfast faith, and sincere concern for them. A strong grasp of the goodness and greatness of God inspired Bonhoeffer throughout his life: in the fruitful years of ministry, in the difficult decision to return to Germany and lead the resistance against Hitler, and in the jail cell before his execution. Thankfulness was his bedrock. He wrote, "In ordinary life we hardly realize that we receive a great deal more than we give, and that it is only with gratitude that life becomes rich."

Celebrating God's character and power reinforces our calling, and celebrating individuals' contributions makes them feel respected and valued. And when we can't find any visible reason to give God thanks and praise, celebration rivets our hearts on his character, reminds us of his sovereignty and goodness, and strengthens our faith when we are tempted to waver. Physiologically, celebrating relieves tension, releases endorphins, and restores a sense of peace. In an organization, a commitment to celebrate reinforces priorities and inspires people to trust God even more. Preaching and teaching about the vision points the way to the future, but celebration says, "That vision is becoming a reality!" It generates tremendous momentum throughout the organization, and ultimately it fosters an even higher and clearer vision of the future because each moment of celebration intuitively tells people, "God has done it once, and he can do it again."

Celebration says, "That vision is becoming a reality!"

HURDLES AND ROADBLOCKS

If celebration has this kind of transforming power, why is it so rare in many churches? Why is it such an area of weakness for most pastors? The answers may be varied and complex, but I am convinced that exhaustion and drivenness are two common factors. Some pastors mistakenly equate exhaustion with commitment, and if they aren't dead tired, they believe they're not giving enough. They never feel as if they've done enough, and they're sure nobody in the church is pleased with them, until they drop dead of terminal tiredness. When we're so tired that we have to drag ourselves through the day, joyful celebration of God's goodness feels like just another thing to check off an already lengthy list of things to do. It's just too much trouble, and besides, we feel more resentment at another task to accomplish than jubilation at God's mercy.

Other leaders are driven by lofty, expansive, God-sized visions that compel them to always strive for more. There are just too many lost people, too many believers not being discipled, and too many unmet needs for them to relax. No matter how many good things God is doing, their eyes stay fixed on the things that remain undone. Larry Osborne, the lead pastor at North Coast Church in Vista, California, calls this the "moving horizon" for visionary pastors. These leaders are always looking at what *might* be, what *could* be, and what (by the grace of God) *will* be. When their church makes progress, they don't waste time sitting around thinking about their success. Instead they push the horizon of possibility out a little further. As admirable as this is in a leader, without the balanced discipline of celebration, this process moves like a conveyor belt. Leaders like this constant progress, but they are so focused on the gap between the possibilities and present successes that they seldom enjoy the fruit God is producing right under their noses.

THE FUTURE

The gap of unmet needs and unreached hopes

DAILY PROGRESS

I'm familiar with this pattern because it describes me — I'm one of those driven pastors. The history of our church is full of monumental answers to prayer and of changed lives that can only be explained by the work of the Spirit, but it's easy for me to forget the past and spend all of my time pressing on to the next major goal, the next big event that promises to meet people's needs, and the next God-sized challenge to reach more lost people, instead of stopping to praise God for all he has done and is doing.

In the lives of visionary leaders, zeal is commendable. We may be wired so that our hearts can run on vision and hope for a long time, but our people need to celebrate progress to stay motivated. Jesus' vision was as high as any has ever been, but he often stopped to relax and celebrate with his followers and friends. I believe that great leaders either have the innate gift of celebration or discipline themselves to develop the habit of gratitude in their lives. Gifted leaders may amaze people with their abilities, their vision of the future, and their soaring rhetoric, but if they never stop to bask in the glory of God's grace and share the joy with others, they may find themselves carrying the vision alone.

Another far more pervasive and insidious problem is our cultural sense of entitlement. It's like a wet blanket on the biblical commands to praise God and give him thanks. In America, we live in the wealthiest and most comfortable society in the history of the world. We enjoy the conveniences of modern technology, have excellent medical care, and can travel in ways that were only dreamed about a generation ago, but we aren't the least bit satisfied. We are stuffed

> We may be wired so that our hearts can run on vision and hope for a long time, but our people need to celebrate progress to stay motivated.

with a sense of entitlement, believing that we deserve even more. The more we gain and acquire, the more we demand. In an interview with Luci Shaw for *Radix* magazine, Dallas Willard, author of *The Divine Conspiracy*, reflected on the impact of rampant consumption in our culture: "We are designed to be creators, initiators, not just receivers. Yet the whole model, the consumerist model of the human being, is [designed] to make us passive, and to make us complainers and whiners, because we're not being given what we need. We cook up a 'right' to that and then we say we've been deprived of our rights. We see this in our churches, which pander to consumers. They say, 'Come and consume the services we offer, and we guarantee you a wonderful time. You'll go out of the church door feeling good.' "[13]

Our discontent flows from a confluence of our selfish natures and the powerful impact of modern advertising, which has a powerful influence on our expectations. The very purpose of advertising is to create discontent. In his book *The Technological Society*, French cultural analyst Jacques Ellul observed,

> One of the great designs of advertising is to create needs; but this is possible only if these needs correspond to an ideal of life that man accepts. The way of life offered by advertising is all the more compelling in that it corresponds to certain

easy and simple tendencies of man and refers to a world in which there are no spiritual values to form and inform life. When men feel and respond to the needs advertising creates, they are adhering to its ideal of life. The human tendencies upon which advertising like this is based may be strikingly simpleminded, but they nonetheless represent pretty much the level of our modern life. Advertising offers us the ideal we have always wanted (and that ideal is certainly not a heroic way of life).[14]

Ellul's insights bring our true motives to light. The ideal life depicted in modern advertising promises to fulfill our expectations of wealth, ease, happiness, and entertainment. In stark contrast, the heroic life is one of honor, duty, sacrifice, and joyful service to others.

Church leaders are not immune to these deceptive messages telling us that we deserve more pleasure, popularity, and possessions. They are the air we breathe every day, and these demands subtly but powerfully distort our values, dreams, and purposes. Daniel Yankelovich, author of the insightful book *New Rules*, observes that in only fifty years, our culture has shifted from self-sacrifice to self-indulgence. The generation that willingly gave their lives to defeat totalitarianism in Germany and Japan would hardly recognize us today. The paralyzing blend of pervasive dissatisfaction and self-indulgence crushes out spiritual life and vitality, but gratitude is a powerful antidote. French philosopher and physicist Blaise Pascal made this recommendation: "Instead of complaining that God has hidden himself, give him thanks for having revealed so much of himself."

> The paralyzing blend of pervasive dissatisfaction and self-indulgence crushes out spiritual life and vitality, but gratitude is a powerful antidote.

STORIES: THE LANGUAGE OF CELEBRATION

All of us have experienced the powerful impact of a great story, the way it connects our heads and our hearts, our understanding and emotions. Good storytelling is also an essential part of celebration and thanksgiving. Some time ago I was thinking about the power of celebration—and my neglect of it—and I decided to carve out time in our staff meetings for everybody to tell stories about how God was working in people's lives. The first week, I explained that God was leading me to emphasize celebration far more, and I wanted us to take thirty minutes in each staff meeting to tell stories about what we'd seen God doing. I invited the staff to begin in that meeting. After a few minutes of awkward silence, one person said something vague about God working so much that people in his ministry group could feel it. "Okay, that's fine," I thought, "but it didn't exactly create a buzz in the room." We waited for the next person to share, and finally someone did. He talked about a specific event he'd held, and he told us the number of people who had come to Christ. "That's cool," I thought, "but it sounded more like an accountant's presentation than a celebration." After a few minutes another person spoke up. He talked about a neighbor for whom he had been praying for six months. They had countless conversations, and he invited his neighbor to church many times. Finally, he told us, his neighbor started attending. Now he prayed even more! And at the invitation to trust Christ the previous Sunday, the staff member peeked and saw his neighbor raise his hand to indicate that he was giving his life to Christ. When the story was finished, each of us had tears in our eyes and a thrill in our hearts!

After a few moments of thanking God for his work in that neighbor's life, I interrupted and asked, "Did you notice what happened? When we heard a story about a person, a relationship, and God's work to transform a life, all of us felt touched. Folks, telling stories is incredibly powerful, but it's hard work. Let's help each other learn to tell great stories."

Create a Culture of Storytelling

God is at work all around us, but before we made storytelling a priority in our staff meetings and in the life of our church, they weren't part of our organizational DNA. We talked about vision, strategies, and needs, but we had to make a special effort (okay, *I* had to make a special effort) to create a culture that truly valued crafting and communicating inspiring stories. To create this culture, we had to make it a regular part of our staff meetings, our casual conversations, and every event at the church. We also had to learn the skills of great storytellers, including:

- Make it specific—give details.
- Make it meaningful—talk about God's work and people's courage.
- Make it short—brevity is the soul of wit and of powerful stories.
- Make it personal—explain how the story impacts you.
- Make it fit your vision and values—and stories of God changing lives always fit.

Have Stories in Your Back Pocket

I used to go through my week of appointments and meetings with a list of agenda items for each encounter, but when I realized the power of stories, I consciously included a recent story to inspire people. The stories, I realized, didn't have to fit the agenda; they just had to be meaningful. Quite often I'll tell someone who walks in my office, "Before we get started, let me tell you about something that happened yesterday," and I'll talk about God touching someone's life. Stories of changed lives inspire people and can transform a bland appointment into a celebration of God's goodness.

Stories of changed lives inspire people and can transform a bland appointment into a celebration of God's goodness.

When our staff team first learned to tell stories, I asked each member to craft one recent, great story about a changed life and tell it in every meeting and appointment all week. I asked them to tell it when they led their small groups, when they met with their ministry leadership teams, to their families, and everywhere they went during the week. I asked them to report back to me at the next staff meeting to tell me how it went.

At the beginning of the next week's meeting, I asked, "How did it go with your stories?" Person after person told how their story had impacted people they met with. And after each person shared, the room erupted in applause and cheers. Do you think that was authentic celebration? Yes, it was the real thing.

One of the staff said that he had gone to family court with a couple in the church, and when he arrived, forty others from the church were there to support them, including the couple's small group and their counselor, who had been meeting with them for months. The judge, our staff member explained, told the packed courtroom, "In all my years on the bench, I've never seen support like this. Who are you people?"

Someone said, "We're from the Oaks Fellowship."

"I've heard of you people," the judge said smiling.

The prosecutor was astonished, and he changed the direction of the case to resolve it without contention.

This tale only took about three minutes to tell, but it fit every criteria of a well-crafted story, and the effect was overwhelming on the rest of us. Even if that had been the only story we heard that day, we would have walked out of there with a renewed sense of what God can do through people who are sold out to him.

Invest in the Craft of Storytelling

In sermons, staff meetings, Bible studies, and meetings with people all day, every day, the point isn't just to tell stories—it's to tell *great* stories, ones that capture people's hearts and inspire them. Some people are natural storytellers, and they have a gift of communicating transforming tales, but the vast majority of us need to put in the hard work to learn the craft. It really is worth the time and effort. I've heard countless messages over the years from pastors who used illustrations they heard in their church history class in seminary or read in *Reader's Digest* a few days before. These are fine, and in a few cases they really grip people, but in my experience the ones people resonate with (and not coincidentally, the ones I enjoy telling) are much more personal and immediate. I love to talk about God touching someone's life yesterday or last week, and I enjoy painting the picture of the moment of transformation. Using stories from history or yesterday's news can be very meaningful, but make sure you connect the point to your listeners today.

Find speakers who tell great stories, and learn from them. You don't need to go to a formal class on the subject, though some of us would surely benefit from one. Listen to gifted storytellers like Chuck Swindoll, John Ortberg, or Andy Stanley. Become a student of the craft. Analyze what makes a story work, and identify the descriptions of emotions, settings, and turning points that make a difference to the hearers. And don't forget to listen too for the crisp, simple, clear point of application when the speaker connects the dots.

As you learn the craft, ask people for feedback, and listen to them. Learning any skill takes time and attention, and it's a process of trial and error. Don't be discouraged if you take a risk and it fails. Learn from it, and do better next time. Above all, tell stories that capture your own heart and thrill your soul. One of the things people love about Chuck Swindoll is his hearty laugh at his own stories. He really enjoys telling them, and we all know it. Ask God to give you empathy for the people in the stories so you can weep with those who weep and rejoice with those who rejoice.

> Above all, tell stories that capture your own heart and thrill your soul.

Tell stories about your own life and your family. People need to hear that you broke the door on the van when your family went on vacation, or that you missed your plane, or you forgot to pick up your mother-in-law (or maybe you didn't really forget!). Remember, when you tell stories about people in your family and your congregation, ask for permission! Almost every week, I call people in our church to ask them if I can use their story. In most cases they're thrilled. Sometimes they ask me to change the names and a few details to keep it anonymous, and occasionally they say no. I always respect their decision, and I never push beyond their comfort level. Thankfully, God has given us such a rich reservoir of terrific stories of changed lives that I seldom have to look very hard for a great illustration.

So ask yourself, "Do I genuinely expect God to be at work in people's lives? Do I see the Spirit's work to rescue the lost, reconcile marriages, turn prodigals and addicts around, and give purpose to those who have been wandering?" Maybe some of us have settled for stories about believers in the dusty pages of church history because we don't see much going on around us. If that's the case, we need far more than the crafting of storytelling skills. We need a heart transplant to trust God for much more than we are experiencing, and we need eye surgery to enable us to see what he's doing in the lives of people we encounter every day.

Use Stories at Every Significant Event to Impart Vision and Enthusiasm

Grand visions of growth capture the hearts of a few people, but stories touch everybody. In fact, if we don't tell stories about individuals' lives when we roll out big new programs, some people will wonder if we're doing it out of pride and the desire to just get bigger. Gripping personal stories remind us of the real reason we do anything big. These stories tell us that our real metric isn't the size of our buildings and budgets but the Spirit's work to change lives one at a time.

Recently we rolled out our vision for the next phase of our church's expansion into our new worship center, and we called it "Experience the Impossible." To put a face to this concept, we videotaped a five-year-old boy whose family moved to our community from the Philippines. He said, "Today I'm being baptized, and I want to live every day for the Lord. My best friend is Shane. He lives next door, and we play every day in his yard or mine. We built the new building for Shane. I wrote his name on the wall when Pastor Scott asked us to write the names of people we hoped would come to Jesus. I've been asking Shane every day to come to church with me, and today he came." He stopped, looked out into the crowd, and waved. "Hi, Shane!" The video ended, and the whole congregation cheered the little boy's faith in God and his love for his friend. To no one's surprise, Shane gave his heart to Christ in the service that day when I gave the invitation.

MULTIPLY YOUR CELEBRATIONS

One of the most beautiful things I've ever seen on our staff team was a shift that occurred soon after our emphasis on storytelling and celebration. In the first week or two, people were getting their sea legs, and they focused primarily on what God was doing in their own ministry areas. Soon, though, I asked them to celebrate what they saw the Lord doing through each other. The next week, a staff member said, "Let me tell you what I saw God doing when I walked through the children's ministry area." He described a specific moment when Vance, our children's pastor, cared for one of the leaders. The cross-ministry affirmation gathered momentum like a snowball rolling downhill. Suddenly everybody started noticing and naming things they saw God doing in each other's ministries and in other churches. Walls of defensiveness and envy came tumbling down, and genuine appreciation for each other grew. Turf wars became a thing of the past (well, that's not entirely true, but they were certainly minimized), and encouragement began to replace envy.

Celebrating God's work in our own lives and ministries was big, but celebrating the Spirit's power at work in each other's ministries was even bigger. But we didn't stop there. The next phase was to focus on the transforming power of praise and thanksgiving, so we celebrated the people who instigate celebration. I told our staff, "I want you to catch each other celebrating God's work in and through other people." The next week, our staff members couldn't wait to talk about what they'd seen in each other in the past few days. One of them said, "I watched as Ron Crane affirmed one of his lay leaders. He did a magnificent job! He was really specific in explaining how he had seen God use Sarah, and he affirmed Sarah's heart and skills. You should have seen the look in her eyes. She soaked up every word!"

You can imagine the impact this had on our staff relationships. Now, instead of each person secretly or overtly jockeying *to be in the spotlight*, each of us wanted *to man the spotlight* to show how God was using others and to celebrate his goodness, greatness, and power in other people's lives. Comparison and jealousy haven't been totally eradicated—that won't happen until Jesus comes back—but in celebration and in celebrating those who celebrate, we've discovered a powerful antidote to those ills. When this becomes a core value of a church, amazing things happen on a staff team, in areas of ministry, throughout the congregation, and in relationships with other churches and organizations. We no longer compete with one another. Instead we delight in becoming "dream releasers" for each other. It's an amazing thing, and it's contagious. Not long ago Dan, our student pastor, spoke at a district youth pastor's conference. When he reported back, in our next staff meeting, about the impact of the district youth director, Justin, one of the staff pastors in the room, sent an email to the DYD to tell him we were bragging on him in our staff meeting. While we were still sitting in the room, the DYD wrote back and said, "Thank you so much for your kind words. As a matter of fact, I was really impressed with the people who came from your church. Your spirit of faith is so obvious. Keep it up!" Justin read the reply to us, and we all thanked God for the privilege of affirming and appreciating each other.

When God's people celebrate each other—on a staff team, in a small group, in a family, or in an entire congregation—a startling transformation occurs. Instead of defending ourselves, we reach out to touch one another with grace. Sometimes this involves the power of physical touch. In his book *Just Like Jesus*, author and pastor Max Lucado observes that our hands have incredible power. He writes, "Oh, the power of our hands. Leave them unmanaged and they become weapons; clawing for power, strangling for survival, seducing for pleasure. But manage them and our hands become instruments of grace—not just tools in the hands of God, but God's very hands. Surrender them and these five-fingered appendages become the hands of heaven."[15]

> Instead of defending ourselves, we reach out to touch one another with grace.

AFFIRM PRIVATELY, PUBLICLY, CONSISTENTLY, AND SPECIFICALLY

If my staff members hear me say from the pulpit, "The staff at this church are the greatest in the world," but I don't affirm them in our meetings and privately, they have every reason to wonder if I'm sincere. Before I ever say anything publicly, I want to be sure to say it privately. This way, people will know I mean it, and sincerity is absolutely essential.

Sometimes affirmation spills out spontaneously as I talk with people. There's nothing wrong with that! But one of the things I've been learning is to prepare messages of affirmation almost as carefully as I prepare sermons. Two traits are necessary for affirmation to be effective: a specific description and authentic appreciation. I think about the personality of the person, and I reflect on the things that have caused the person's eyes to light up in the past. I consider the details of the event or character quality I want to highlight, and carefully choose words that have the most meaning for that person.

If I've affirmed my staff members privately and in a staff meeting, they'll believe me when I tell the whole church how much I appreciate them. And of course I try to affirm as many people in our church as possible. Love builds trust and respect wherever it's communicated. I try to tell people often and sincerely how much I love them and appreciate them. As much as possible, I try to catch them doing things for the Lord so I can thank them. My role as their pastor is a sacred position, one they value very highly, and so my words matter to them. I've had scores of people in our church tell me how much my meager efforts to affirm them and communicate love have meant to them—and the look in their eyes means the world to me.

DOUBLE YOUR EMPHASIS ON CELEBRATION DURING TRANSITIONS

Periods of transition and chaos are enormously stressful. If we're not careful, the strain will erode our energy, and friction between people will rub off the sharp edge of our passion. Celebration isn't optional at any time, but it's especially important in times of transition—times when we're tempted to neglect it because we're so focused on the future and on solving problems to get there.

Make a special effort to build praise, thanksgiving, and affirmation into your life, into your staff meetings, and into every facet of your ministry during times of transition. Celebration generates the energy you need to keep going, refocuses your heart on what's most important, crystallizes your faith on the character and purposes of God, and relieves tons of stress. When you feel stretched to the limit, you can't afford to neglect celebration.

> When you feel stretched to the limit, you can't afford to neglect celebration.

Let's be honest. There are times in all of our lives when the last thing we want to do is celebrate. We want to gripe, blame others, and feel sorry for ourselves, and sometimes we just want to give up and leave the ministry because it's just too hard. In the most difficult moments, we need to find one thing, just one, for which we can thank God. We don't have to feel all warm and tingly inside about the Spirit's work, but we have to find a single, bedrock truth about the character of God or about the faith of a friend or the love of a spouse or the purpose of God—something, anything, about which we can say, "God, thank you for this." Start there and see what happens in the coming days and weeks. I believe God delights in us coming to him and clinging to him no matter how small our faith may seem at the moment. If we'll come, he'll honor our seed of trust. We may not have a flash of relief and strength at that moment or on the next day or even in the next month, but it'll come. Sometimes he wants us to wait for him, but waiting isn't just killing time. The admonition to "wait for the LORD" (Ps. 27:14) means to expect him to be himself and work in his way, in his time, and for his purposes, to not put any restrictions on him or demand that he act in a certain way but hold tight to him because we're convinced that he knows, he cares, and he will eventually have his way in our lives.

MAPPING YOUR DIRECTION

1. From your own experience, describe the power of celebration to transform your perspective, strengthen relationships, reinforce vision, and give a sense of peace.

2. How does each of the following roadblocks act as a wet blanket on celebration?

   - Exhaustion:
   - Drivenness:
   - A sense of entitlement:

3. How well do you and your church celebrate? How would an objective outside observer evaluate your ability to celebrate?

4. Pick three of the following suggestions for storytelling and write a brief plan to implement them.

   - Create a culture of storytelling.
   - Have stories in your back pocket.
   - Invest in the craft of storytelling.
   - Use stories at every significant event to impart vision and enthusiasm.

5. After reading this chapter and reflecting on the importance of celebrating, what is one thing you want God to do in your own heart to help you lead more authentically and effectively in this area?

6. Mark your calendar right now to carve out time to talk as a staff and board to share some of the incredible stories of what God is doing in your church.

CHAPTER 8

THE LEADERSHIP GAP

Finding a Great Coach

We must make the choices that enable us to fulfill the deepest capacities of our real selves. — THOMAS MERTON

Pastors will quote passages in Ephesians and Philippians about the beauty of the body of Christ working together in harmony. They will quote Jesus and John about the power of love. They can preach eloquently about the proverb that says, "He who walks with the wise grows wise, but a companion of fools suffers harm" (Prov. 13:20). But many pastors remain some of the most isolated and lonely people in the world. Day in and day out they hear about the crushing problems in people's lives, but they don't have anyone they can be honest with about their own struggles. The pressure builds, and eventually many experience burnout.

I know how this feels. I was one of them.

A number of years ago, when I served under my father, I was haunted by dreams of him dying and leaving me with the responsibility of the ministry. These nightmares combined the two most painful and threatening things I could imagine. As the weeks passed, the normal stresses of ministry seemed to multiply, and none of my daily activities brought me any joy or satisfaction. For a year and a half I dreaded Sundays. You know there's a problem when a pastor says the worst day of his week is Sunday! People called me during the week to tell me they were bringing a friend, neighbor, or family member to church this week to hear the gospel, and I felt tremendous pressure to deliver. I thought, "I'd better not blow it, or that person will go to hell." Normal staff problems looked like Mount Everest, and normal budget difficulties felt like the end of the world.

I thought I was doing a great job hiding all my anxieties, but then I realized that my reactions to staff, family, friends, and everyone who breathed were sharp and angry. Jesus teaches us that "out of the overflow of the heart the mouth speaks" (Matt. 12:34). My heart was abundantly full of fear, anger, doubt, hurt, and self-pity, and the overflow wasn't pretty! I may have preached about the peace of Christ, but it was a foreign concept to me at the time.

Near Christmas that year, all I wanted to do was be alone, but when you're a pastor, that's not a convenient time to suddenly become a hermit! Family members wanted to talk to me, but I avoided them. People called to tell me, "Merry Christmas," but I felt like the modern manifestation of Ebenezer Scrooge. My wife, Jenni, and our boys wanted to spend time with me, but even casual interaction felt like a burden I couldn't bear. Finally Jenni looked at me and said, "Scott, you need to get some help." She was right.

Because of my life coach, I'm a better pastor, husband, and father.

Immediately I went on a search for a gifted Christian counselor who could help me maneuver through the emotional craziness I was feeling. God blessed me with a man who has been a true gift to me. He helped me during that turbulent time years ago, and I've continued to see him because he enables me to sort out so much of the confusion and distractions I face as a leader. Because of him, I'm a better pastor, husband, and father. I don't know where I'd be today if it weren't for the insight and help I receive from him when we meet every other week. He's a major part of the support structure God has given me that allows me to continue to move forward in times of chaos.

THE KIND OF FRIEND WE NEED

Many pastors may have friends they can talk to, but I want to raise the bar even several notches higher. The kind of friend we need isn't just a buddy who listens, empathizes, and pats us on the back. We need friends like that for lunches and ball games, but at times we also need a professional who has the wisdom to grasp what's going on in our lives. Someone who doesn't have any agenda for us or a conflict of interest in giving advice. We need someone who is objective, skilled, insightful—and paid. My life coach doesn't have a vested interest in the church; he has a vested interest in me. To avoid a sticky conflict of interests, I looked for someone outside our church who wouldn't try to give me advice so that the youth ministry or the worship team or any other ministry would benefit from the input he gave me. I wanted someone who was totally devoted first to Christ and his kingdom, and second to my development as a leader. Nothing else and nothing less.

Dr. Samuel Chand is my life coach. He calls himself a dream releaser, and that's exactly the role he plays in my life. Let me describe the role in more detail.

An Accurate Mirror

I don't know how many times I thought I had something all figured out, but when I talked to Dr. Chand, he would ask questions that totally changed my understanding and direction. It was sort of like looking in a mirror and being surprised to see a big blob of dirt on my cheek. The blob had been there all along, but until I looked in the mirror, I just didn't see it. I talk to Dr. Chand about everything in my life: from my overall life direction and long-term goals to some of the smallest details of my plans. Dr. Chand believes in the benefit of self-discovery, so instead of just telling me the right answers, he asks good questions that teach me how to dig and discover the answers for myself. Our church is truly a different place because these questions have powerfully shaped my thinking. From the very first day Dr. Chand and I met, I could tell that God has given him unusual insight into people and organizations, and I trust him to speak the truth to me—to be an accurate mirror of reality.

A Vision Stretcher

I didn't look for someone whose ministry was at the same level as my own. Earlier I recommended that we get input from churches that are three times larger than our own. In this way, we gain the expertise of their greater vision and experience. In the same manner, I wanted a life coach who has been to places I've never been, so he could stretch my vision to include possibilities I'd never consider on my own. Dr. Chand certainly fits the bill. Sometimes I think I'm at the ultimate limit of growth possibilities, but Dr. Chand pushes me to think bigger. He has helped in every phase of strategic planning, from concept to fine-tuning. And because he knows me so well, his affirmations mean the world to me. I appreciate it when others say, "You're doing a great job," but it means even more when Dr. Chand reviews my plans, hears my heart, and says, "Pastor Scott, you're on the right track."

Sometimes we need to be pushed and we don't even know it.

Sometimes we need to be pushed and we don't even know it. Not long after we moved into our first building at the Oaks Fellowship, we had grown by about three hundred. I thought we were doing really well. In one of my meetings with Dr. Chand in January after the move, he asked, "How much money do you need this year beyond your regular giving?"

I thought for a minute before I answered. I didn't want to sound as if my vision was limited, but we had just moved into our new facility, and we had asked people for money plenty of times. One more request, I felt, would be too much. I didn't want to become known as the preacher who only asked for money. Finally I answered, "About two hundred and fifty thousand dollars."

Dr. Chand leaned across the table and said, "Pastor Scott, I don't mean this month. I mean this year."

We both chuckled . . . kind of. I knew where he was going. He then asked, "What projects need to be funded?"

"We need to complete the parking lot, and we need to work on our drainage."

"How much would that cost?" he asked.

"Well," I began to explain, "we can probably cover one of our needs by the end of the year with the two hundred and fifty thousand."

"Not one of them. All of them."

"All of them?"

He smiled. "Yes, all of them."

I quickly calculated the numbers in my head. "We'd need about six hundred thousand dollars."

"Then that's the number you need to trust God to provide and ask your people to give," he told me confidently.

He could see me squirm, so he explained, "Pastor Scott, you can raise all that money in the next ten weeks."

Now I was really squirming! I told him, "Dr. Chand, I don't mean to be disrespectful. I know you've had a lot of experience, but there's no way we can raise that kind of money."

He wouldn't be deterred. He continued, "Easter is coming up in a few weeks, and I have an idea about how to raise that money." I was still hesitant, so he looked at me and asked, "Do you trust me, Pastor Scott?"

"Yes," I answered a bit awkwardly. "I trust you."

"Then let me help you do what God has called you to do." He outlined a plan to ask people for money during the next few weeks and then announce the results on Easter Sunday.

We implemented the plan, and on Easter Sunday we had raised $475,000. It wasn't quite all we were shooting for, but it was almost double the amount I had hoped to raise during the entire year. I was really excited when I called Dr. Chand to tell him the news. I think I could hear him smile too.

The next January he asked me the same question again. This time I had a bigger number in mind, but again he blew me out of the water with a bigger vision of what God could do. He said, "The money has been there all along. People want to give. You just need eyes to see it. The biggest limitation to this church's growth is the ceiling of your faith. You need God to stretch your faith even more." Before I started spending time with Dr. Chand, I used to think I was a man of great vision, but soon I realized I had a lot to learn.

A Gifted Strategist

I devour books about church growth. I think I've read every word that Bill Hybels and Andy Stanley have ever written, and

I've read the books or listened to talks by the sharpest minds in modern evangelicalism. In addition, books like Jim Collins' *Good to Great* have inspired and challenged me. I'm a sponge for input, and I benefit from Dr. Chand's wisdom to apply principles to our specific situation at the Oaks Fellowship and to my leadership style. For example, Collins' "Hedgehog Concept" explains the importance of having a central, unifying, "simple, crystalline concept that flows from a deep understanding ... of three questions: What can you be the best in the world at? What drives your economic engine? And, what are you deeply passionate about?"[16] Dr. Chand helped me grasp the nuances of applying this principle to the church culture, and specifically to *our* church's culture.

> A life coach brings a wealth of experience and insight to you and can help you adjust your plans to capitalize on the opportunities God has given you.

A life coach brings a wealth of experience and insight to you and can help you adjust your plans to capitalize on the opportunities God has given you. This input and feedback throughout the process of conceptualizing, planning, and implementing inspires confidence and yields tremendously fruitful results.

A Trusted Confidant

From time to time God makes me aware of darkness in my heart that scares me. I don't want anybody to know it's there, but if I try to suppress it, the negative, selfish thoughts seem to multiply. At one point I started comparing myself with some successful pastors I know. It began when a friend praised a pastor whose church was really successful, and envy began to take root in my heart. I was going to meet with Dr. Chand, and I thought about telling him about it. If I told him, I risked losing his respect, but if I didn't, I knew that this secret could drive a hidden wedge between us. I decided to tell him, and I poured out my heart to him. When I was finished, I asked, "What do I do with all that?"

I waited anxiously for his reply, and he said, "Pastor Scott, just speaking it out loud takes the power away from it. When we harbor those things as secrets, they have enormous power to control us and destroy us, but when we speak them to someone we trust, the power vanishes." And he was right. His understanding and acceptance immediately caused my shame to evaporate, and I felt tremendous relief.

If we try to process a deep level of our pain and doubt with others in the church, we risk inappropriate exposure, and we can make it difficult for our confidant to trust us, because he may not expect us to have real problems in our lives. Senior pastors are especially vulnerable. Everyone in the church reports directly or indirectly to them, and they put themselves and others at risk by disclosing too much about themselves. But leaders can't keep stuffing those painful thoughts and feelings week after week and expect them to go away. They need to find someone who is

> Leaders can't keep stuffing those painful thoughts and feelings week after week and expect them to go away.

KNOW WHO TO LISTEN TO

Troy Grambling
Flamingo Road Church: Cooper City, Florida

In 2002 I accepted the lead pastor position at Flamingo Road Church. As the church transitioned under my new leadership, the biggest challenge I faced was dealing with the people who were leaving. This happened in three waves and ranged from nominal attenders I really didn't know to several pastors I greatly loved and trusted. The first wave that left the church were folks who left because of the shift in leadership. As the church began to look more like who God made me to be and less like their former pastor, they decided they didn't fit with the changes. Fortunately, as they left, many new people (excited about the new vision) came. Eventually the back door closed, and we began to see some amazing numerical growth.

In 2004 we experienced our second wave of loss. We faced huge financial challenges due to the completion of a new auditorium (an auditorium that had been under construction before I became lead pastor). Our debt service, after completion of the auditorium, represented almost 50 percent of our monthly giving. Consequently, we had to let go of about 25 percent of our staff and make

continued on next page...

some large budget reductions. A couple of years later, due to rapid growth, we faced our third wave of loss. This wave was gut-wrenching for me. Some of our staff had hit their leadership lid, and as a result, we had to say goodbye to some of our closest friends. Through all of this, I had to continue pushing forward, even in the midst of pain; my challenge was to not let myself be led *by* my pain but to lead *through* my pain. There is great danger in leading *by* your pain, because you can become vengeful, doubtful, and insecure. Leading *by* your pain will paralyze your leadership. But I sought God desperately during this time, and I realized that the church (and my calling to lead it) must move forward. Through all of these changes, I've learned an important lesson. Be careful who you choose to listen to during times of transition!

I boiled it down to three groups of people that I listen to when I need advice or encouragement:

1. *Those who love me.* They may not understand the vision (yet), but they love me as a person.
2. *Those who believe in me.* They believe our vision is God-breathed and God-ordained and believe I am the person God has raised up to carry it out.
3. *Those who know more than me.* They may not love me, they may not know the vision, but they simply know more than me.

Seeing people leave our church will always be a challenge for me. However, through this season of ministry, I learned a lot about myself and grew closer to God — two priceless lessons that will certainly help me whenever a season like this rolls in again.

objective, caring, and wise so they can spill out all the ugliness, gain perspective and hope, and move forward.

Dr. Chand advised me to avoid going into the office on my worst days. I don't have to say I'm struggling or in a bad mood; I simply work from my office in my home. If I go to the office on those days, I may have noble motives, but the abundance of negativity in my heart can easily overflow and harm other people. Out of love for them, I don't want that to happen. (Of course, this should only be a rare course of action. If this becomes a pattern, I need to get more help.)

A Pace Setter

I've known lots of church leaders who wear stress as a badge of honor. The more they can complain about having too much to do, being misunderstood and underappreciated, and dealing with the difficulties of managing God's work on limited resources, the better they feel about themselves. That's ridiculous, and it can lead to dangerous consequences.

In his book *Margin: Restoring Emotional, Physical, Financial and Time Reserves to Our Overloaded Lives,* physician Richard Swenson teaches that moderate levels of stress actually bring out the best in us by stimulating our creativity and motivating us to pursue bigger visions. But as with the frog in the kettle, stress can increase so gradually that we don't perceive the effects. When high levels of stress become normal in our lives, we fail to notice and make changes. Then our abilities erode, our capacities shrink, we are more distracted and rushed, so we make bad decisions, and our relationships suffer—all of which adds even more stress to the situation. If we experience extreme stress for a long period of time, we face the devastation of burnout.[17]

If we are in the midst of transition and chaos, everyone feels additional pressure, and either they look to us to relieve it or they blame us for it. In that environment, we simply must learn to handle stress before it takes us to the breaking point. There's no shame in living a balanced life, in carving out time to think, laugh, and enjoy the ones we love—and even to play golf once in a while. Instead of feeling proud of carrying a huge burden of stress, we need to see that attitude as pathological. To make the shift, we need a life coach to speak truth and grace into our lives. Left on my own, I simply can't distinguish between the important and the urgent, but with some wise input, priorities become much clearer.

A Wise Counselor

Visionary leadership necessarily involves a strange blend of certainty and ambiguity. I know where God is calling us, but I have no idea how he's going to provide the people, finances, and strategies to get there. Staff transitions always include a blend of decisions and unanswered questions. And family life is the same way. Every parent knows the difficulty of figuring out how to raise children, raising multiple children with very different personalities, and raising teenagers who are still under our roofs but insist on being treated like adults.

Visionary leadership necessarily involves a strange blend of certainty and ambiguity.

We will grow only to the level of our pain threshold, and that threshold can be characterized by our willingness to admit, "I don't know." For years I thought I had to have all the answers, and to be honest, if someone asked and I didn't know, I often made something up. Sometimes it sounded pretty good, but sometimes they saw right through me. For the sake of our own heart and to build trust with those who follow us, we need to be willing to say, "I don't know, but let's trust God together for an answer."

GETTING THE MOST OUT OF THE RELATIONSHIP

A support system is only as effective as the leader's ability to internalize the input. My time with Dr. Chand has incredible power to shape my life because I invest so much into our time and I apply what I learn. We meet once a month for four to six hours. Before every meeting, I put in about four hours of reflection and planning. I write a report about the steps we agreed on last month and the things I've done to implement them. I list the questions I want to ask about the items on the agenda, plus any other questions I want to talk about with him. I send this report and my questions to him several days before he arrives, so that he can be thinking, praying, and planning for our meeting.

I treasure our time together. My life is so much richer because God brought Dr. Chand into it. Our church pays his consulting and coaching fees, and it's the best money we spend out of our budget. Every facet of our ministry benefits from my time with him, and every person is directly or indirectly stronger.

Some pastors will say, "Well, that's great for you, but our church can't afford to pay a life coach for me." My answer is that your church can't afford not to. The benefits are worth far more than the costs—but you have to find the right person.

THE RIGHT PROFILE

Most of us don't know what kind of person we need as our life coach. I suggest that you talk to pastors who have one, and develop a profile of the person who matches you and your needs. When you know what you're looking for, you're much more likely to find the right person. You've heard the old saying, "When the student is ready, the teacher will appear." This principle applies in many areas of life. When our minds have a clear template of expectations, we notice and sort options far more effectively.

Life coaching is one of the hottest phenomena in the executive world today. Many corporations hire coaches for their top execs because they're convinced the investment pays enormous dividends. In the church world, some counselors have converted their practices to coaching, and some in the executive coaching field who are believers devote their skills to pastors and Christian executives in business. To find the right match, consider these criteria:

- What are your greatest needs? (Planning, leading a diverse staff team, finances, personal development, crisis counseling, etc.)
- What are the needs of your church? (Which stage of the sigmoid curve is it in? What are the opportunities and obstacles you face today? What will you face a year from now?)
- What are your strengths? What are areas of need in your leadership?
- As you build trust with the life coach, will you be willing to take off your mask and be real with him or her?
- What are the tangible benefits you are seeking from a life coach?

As you analyze coaches, look for the best fit. Consider these traits:

- *Expertise and experience.* In what field does the person have experience and training? Does this person have the ability to take you to the place God wants you to go? Has he or she already been there?
- *Credentials.* Does the person have a graduate-level degree or certification in the field in which you need help?
- *Exposure to church work.* Does the person grasp the nuances of church leadership?
- *Cultural fit.* Does this person's experience fit culturally with your situation?
- *Availability.* Is the person you want booked already? Will he or she become available soon?
- *Face-to-face or by phone.* Some coaches offer sessions by phone. Is this what you want, or do you prefer face time?
- *Personality.* Do you like and respect this person?
- *Frequency.* How often does the coach want to meet?
- *Preparation.* What are the coach's expectations about reflection, planning, and implementation of each session's conclusions and plans?
- *Promises.* What does this person promise to do for you? Pay close attention to this statement, and refer back to it during the course of coaching to make sure you stay on track.
- *Fees.* Are they reasonable?
- *Termination.* What kind of termination agreement are you asked to sign?

JUST GET STARTED

I didn't ask Dr. Chand to be my personal coach at the beginning. This role evolved out of him consulting with the church. We hired him to come to the Oaks Fellowship to help us clarify our direction and strategy. He met for four hours with me, and then he met with about twenty of our top leaders. For several weeks he processed all of the information gleaned from these meetings, and then he came back to give us a report. I picked up Dr. Chand at the airport, and we went to the nearby Barnes & Noble that served as our "office" for three years. He opened his notebook, and two hours later he finished the last of thirty-eight specific recommendations that would help us become the church we believed God wanted us to be. The changes he proposed were so sweeping that I was blown away. I had tears in my eyes, not because I was so excited but because I was devastated. I told him, "I don't think I can do this. I don't think I'm capable."

He reached across the table and put his hand on mine the way a father would touch his struggling son, and he said, "Hey, I've been through this a hundred times. You can do it, and I'll help you." After my head cleared a bit, I took his offer. I asked him if he'd become my coach and mentor, and he graciously agreed.

"Hey, I've been through this a hundred times. You can do it, and I'll help you."

You won't get very far down the road unless you're willing to take a first step. You may want to hire a consultant for the church and see where it goes, or you may want to talk to a friend who recommends a life coach for you. You may have a thousand questions about how the relationship will work, and you may wonder how much of your fears and doubts to share with that person. Those misgivings are perfectly normal, but don't let them stop you. Ask the Lord for wisdom, talk to a friend or two who use life coaches, go online to find some in your area, and dive in. If the first one doesn't work out as well as you hoped, it's not a marriage. Graciously exit the relationship and find someone else.

Depending on the size and nature of your staff team, I recommend a life coach for every member of your executive team (for a large staff team) or every staff member (for a small team). Start with the senior pastor, but don't stop there. In a few months help the next tier of staff to find coaches who fit them and their needs, but don't use a cookie-cutter approach. The members of your team may have very different strengths and needs, so help them find coaches who can address their unique situations. Finding coaches for your team costs money, but in my experience it's the best money your church can spend, because it maximizes your effectiveness as individuals and as a team.

This may surprise you, but I believe that of all the principles in this book, hiring a life coach is the most significant one I've learned and applied—hands down. If you don't do anything else I suggest in these pages, find a life coach. It can make all the difference in the world for you, your family, your staff, your leadership team, your congregation, and the lost people in your community who need Christ. It's that important.

When our lives change because of the benefits of interacting with a life coach, we can pass along the blessings to others. Today I'm a coach for four pastors. I use the principles and methods I've learned from Dr. Chand with these men, and I thoroughly enjoy meeting with them. Someday they will probably become coaches too, and the legacy will multiply.

MAPPING YOUR DIRECTION

1. Pastors and other leaders are around people all the time. Why, do you think, do so many feel isolated and lonely?

2. On a scale of zero to ten, how much do you want and need a life coach to help you with the following issues? Explain your answer.

   • An accurate mirror
   • A vision stretcher
   • A gifted strategist
   • A trusted confidant
   • A pacesetter
   • A wise counselor

3. What would it take for your board to value the benefits of a life coach and spend the money to hire one for you?

4. Briefly review your needs and a life coach's qualifications in the section called "The Right Profile." Which factors in both parts of this section stand out to you?

5. Is my statement that finding a life coach is the most important principle in this book surprising to you? Why or why not?

6. What's your next step in finding the right life coach? What's your timeline for finding this person and beginning the relationship?

Note: If you are a senior pastor and you'd like more information on finding a life coach, you can contact me at scottwilson@ scottwilsonleadership.org.

CHAPTER 9

KEEP THE VISION FRESH

Vision helps leaders get people very different from one
another to pull together for a common purpose. Failure to
build shared vision is the biggest mistake that
gifted leaders make. — BILL EASUM

In times of transition, people often confuse vision and strategy. In chaos, long-used systems and schedules have to be reevaluated. Some of them undergo major surgery, and a few need to be eliminated to make room for new plans. Many people, though, feel that the old wineskins worked just fine, and they are extremely reluctant to try new ones. During these times, leaders have to patiently and persistently communicate the difference between an ironclad vision and the strategies that need to be flexible to reach new goals. The vision doesn't change, but the vehicle to get there may change dramatically.

I heard a speaker once explain it this way: If you want to travel from Red Oak, Texas, to London, England, you can take one of two routes. You can drive to the Dallas/Fort Worth airport and hop on a direct flight, or you can drive to New York and take a ship. You have two options, but both involve changing vehicles to reach your destination. In either scenario, if you insist on staying in the car, you simply can't get to London. You can either change your vehicle (how to get there) or change your vision (where you want to go).

> If people become too attached to existing vehicles and forget the vision, they'll drag their feet as you try to lead them through transition.

As we implement the vision God has called us to achieve, we need to help people fix their eyes on the ultimate goal and then learn to change vehicles whenever it's necessary. If people become too attached to existing vehicles and forget the vision, they'll drag their feet as you try to lead them through transition. This was our experience as we went through the transition process.

VISION AND VEHICLE AT THE OAKS FELLOWSHIP

Since our church began, Sunday school has been an important part of our strategy for making fully devoted followers of Christ. God has given us wonderful teachers who creatively, enthusiastically, and practically impart his truth to over a thousand people each week. I realize that many churches today don't have a Sunday school program, and it's not necessarily the coolest or most current strategy, but it has fit our values and culture from the first day, and God has used this ministry to change many lives.

When we entered chaos several years ago to anticipate the next phase of growth, we planned to build our new building so that we could reach more people in our community. In our planning, we had to carefully examine the three major bottlenecks to our growth: parking, childcare, and seats in the worship center. Early on we realized that if we added five hundred to one thousand more people, we'd have a corresponding increase in children needing childcare. Where could we put these kids? We couldn't cram them into the existing space—it was already crowded. (We thought about building a corral in the field behind the new building, but we didn't think that would send the right message to the newcomers!) I asked our staff to brainstorm ideas for using our space most effectively, and they came back with a report saying that our projected needs for childcare would use most of the rooms we were currently using for Sunday school. For six weeks we spent time in every staff meeting trying to keep the Sunday school classes intact and still find places for all the children. In each of these staff meetings, we began by looking at each week's new report in silence and then hashing out every conceivable option. The hard truth was slowly sinking in: We'd have to find another way to accomplish our educational goals. This was going to require a major change in vehicles!

I met with each of the teachers, and I told them how we had carefully analyzed the situation, wrestled with the logistics, and concluded that we'd have to find a new way of doing Christian education at our church. They weren't mad, and nobody got up and yelled or fussed. But they were visibly saddened. I promised them that we would look for a creative solution because we weren't going to waste their talents, gifts, passion, and experience.

As word of this decision spread around the church, I began to hear rumors of discontent—not from the teachers but from others who hadn't been at the meeting. A couple of them confronted me. One man said, "Pastor, I wasn't too upset when we stopped having Sunday night services so we could start small groups. That was fine. But not having Sunday school? That's a different deal. I want to go to a church that values discipleship, and it's obvious ours doesn't value discipleship anymore. I'm thinking about going to another church." Another man told me, "I hear we're not going to do discipleship anymore, so I have an idea: our mission is to lead people to Jesus, and then we can send them to other churches that disciple people. What do you think of that?"

I explained that we weren't abandoning discipleship. It was still central to our vision. We were just changing strategics. My conversations with these gentlemen, like those with countless others during times of chaos, illustrate the necessity of helping people distinguish between vision and vehicle, mission and method. Just because we were changing our Sunday school strategy didn't mean we were devaluing discipleship. Not in the least. In fact, my hope was to find an even better way to disciple people.

There was one lady, though, who demonstrated true faith during this transition. She had been a Christian for several years, and she had watched our church go through transitions and chaos before. During the darkest of those days, after I told the teachers that we weren't doing Sunday school any longer, but before we had any new plans in place, she came up to me after church, leaned up, and gave me a kiss on the cheek. As she hugged me, she whispered, "Pastor Scott, it's going to be all right. Don't you worry. God is going to provide a way." She had no idea how much I appreciated her faith in God and her trust in me as her pastor.

I asked several of our top leaders to meet during the next several weeks to come up with an answer. This team included the director of our discipleship ministries and the directors of our children's ministry, student ministries, adult assimilation, and small groups. They knew how much we had anguished over this decision, and they knew many dear people were looking to them for God's answer to the problem. I asked them not to just come up with an answer but to trust God for a superior strategy, something that would go far beyond anything we'd ever imagined. It was a God-sized request.

Six weeks later they presented their plan to me, and together we met with our teachers. The plan is a comprehensive discipleship strategy that includes four components:

1. Worship services teach the Scriptures to the broad audience that attends our church. These are catalyst events full of "God moments," when he touches people and they make life-changing decisions to follow him.

2. Small groups offer a powerful blend of community, care, and Bible teaching. The groups study the topic taught in the sermon each week, and we give people study guides to help them dig deeper into the Scriptures and prepare for their small group interactions. Michael Brown, our small groups pastor, incorporates additional insights, passages, and questions in the guide. His contributions add immeasurably to the power of our small group experience.

3. One-on-one discipleship modules are offered in person and online. These cover a wide range of topics, including: grounding new believers in the faith; finances; marriage; parenting; finding purpose in life; and many other areas of specific application of biblical truth. At our church, someone who is discipling a friend can direct him or her to a series on the website, and when the friend finishes the written part of each lesson, the two of them can meet at a

local coffee shop or in one of their homes to complete the relational component of the lesson.

4. The Pastoral Leadership Institute is an invitation-only teaching and training series that meets once a month to equip rising leaders with vision, ministry philosophy, skills training, and other aspects of development.

WORSHIP SERVICES

SMALL GROUPS

ONE-ON-ONE
DISCIPLESHIP MODULES

THE PASTOR'S
LEADERSHIP INSTITUTE

To say the least, God had answered our prayers for a superior strategy! Our teachers saw they could participate in leading small groups locally, and they could help craft the curriculum for the one-on-one modules. Actually, they saw even more potential in the new strategy than did any of those who had crafted it! One teacher said, "Because the modules will be online, our friends in Scotland can use it in their church." Another connected the dots and told us, "I'd like to use the modules in the small group I'm leading." Someone else remarked, "I have friends who go to other churches. They don't have anything like this, but they can get ours online." Others realized that their gifts in teaching would now allow them to touch people's lives as we expanded to multisite campuses, and through the magic of the internet, to churches on an even broader scale. As we talked, the lights came on, and someone said, "There are churches of one hundred or two hundred people all over the world who don't have good discipleship material. God might use us to equip them!"

Our vision for teaching and equipping believers hadn't changed, but our vehicle had changed drastically. In the past, people had equated Sunday school with discipleship, and they couldn't imagine doing away with these classes. It felt as if we were throwing out the whole idea of discipleship. Now they realized that our new strategy would enable them to have a greater impact on far more people. For years people could only be taught, trained, and equipped if they came to classes that were scheduled in a specific place at a particular time. With our new strategy, all of the restraints were cast off, and the doors were wide open to new possibilities. In trusting God for this strategy, the leaders of the Oaks Fellowship had experienced the impossible. Now people all over the world would benefit from God's work through these teachers. But the old wineskins had to be discarded before God led us to find new ones.

> The old wineskins had to be discarded before God led us to find new ones.

As our Sunday school teachers grasped the significance of this new strategy, they got really excited about the part they could play in making it a reality. In a single meeting, a superior strategy washed away the gloom and replaced it with passion, vision, and a renewed trust in the leadership of our church.

Not bad. Not bad at all.

EVERY DIFFICULTY IS A TEST

Many people have asked me why I didn't wait until we had the new plans in place before we told our teachers that we were changing our strategy. Certainly, I would have preferred that course of action, but it wasn't an option for one simple reason: God hadn't given us the new plans yet! I knew that I needed to speak the truth to our teachers. The worst thing I could do would be to hide what I knew, that Sunday school as we knew it would cease to exist. Like Abraham, I chose to take the first step without knowing where we were going, but I needed to tell them at least where we *weren't* going. After taking this step, I could enlist our leaders to pray and trust God for a better solution.

I knew God would give us a better strategy; I just didn't know what it would be. I was convinced that God cares far more about teaching and training his people than any of us do. I just didn't

CHANGING LEADERSHIP

Randall Ross
Calvary Church: Naperville, Illinois

In July of 1967 my friend Bob Schmidgall founded Calvary Church in Naperville, Illinois. He served as senior pastor until his untimely death in 1998. Along with his wife, Karen, and a team of eight Bible college students, Bob founded the church and saw it grow to an attendance of over two thousand.

Many years ago at a meeting Bob said to me, "Randal, someday you will pastor my church." Never in my wildest dreams did I realize that the Lord was giving Bob insight into the future of Calvary Church — not to mention my own future in ministry! After Bob unexpectedly passed away, Calvary Church was without a senior pastor for over two years. During that time the church not only survived but thrived under the capable leadership of the staff and outside speakers. In January of 2000, just as Bob had predicted, I was invited to be the senior pastor of Calvary Church.

While I was honored and excited to assume the leadership of such a great church, I was well aware of the challenges I was facing. When a pastor follows the founding pastor of a successful and growing church, that person needs wisdom and discernment as he leads the congregation — especially when they have only known one pastor and one style of leadership. Many of the people in Calvary's congregation had come to know Christ because of Bob, had been married and had had family members buried by Bob, and had known only one man as their pastor. Thankfully, in my previous pastorates, God taught me many things that had prepared me for this transition in the life of the church.

Here are a few principles that I've found helpful when navigating transitions in ministry, particularly when you are following another pastor. First, be secure in the fact that God has called you to lead the congregation. While we praise God for the past, the church must be focused on the future. I knew that God had called me to take lead of this church, and I was careful to affirm the past without allowing the congregation to live there. I was able to do this because of my confidence that God had called me to lead the church. Too often pastors are insecure about the successes of previous pastors. But if we are truly grounded in our calling and focused on building the kingdom of God, we can be secure and rejoice in the past while presenting a fresh vision for the future.

Second, as much as possible, work with the present staff and leadership. Pastors frequently come in with the mindset to change the staff rather than

continued on next page…

work with those who have faithfully served the congregation and held the church together during the time of transition. The existing staff will be the stable glue between you and the former pastor. If at all possible, it is important to keep the team together for the sake of the congregation.

Third, be slow to implement change. Obviously, styles and ideas are different. Bob and I had very different leadership styles, different philosophies for ministry, and even different teaching styles. People are naturally going to compare you with the way things used to be, so as much as possible (even if it goes against your personality), resist changing things right away; instead introduce change slowly. People tend to like things the way they are. Once they have accepted you as their leader, you will have greater freedom to introduce changes over time. Your people will more willingly accept the changes that you need to bring, but be patient.

Finally, a leader needs to understand the cultural identity of the church. Calvary Church had a certain identity and culture that had existed for over thirty years, and for two years there had been no senior leadership, so very little had changed. As I approached the senior pastorate, I was careful to appreciate the traditions of Calvary and did my best to help people see areas where we needed to change. A common mistake that new pastors make is to violate the culture of the church by always suggesting that there is a better way to do things. Sometimes it's just a matter of perspective. Your way might not be better, just different. Remember that changing a culture is the most challenging step in transitioning into a new pastorate. Be sure to listen to key influencers and the community around your church so you can better understand the cultural identity of your congregation.

These principles, along with God's help, have allowed us to carry forward Bob's dream at Calvary Church and to see the church continue to have an impact in Naperville and throughout the world. Regardless of your transitional situation, these simple steps can help you navigate the changes you'll need to make to pursue the vision God has given you as a leader.

know when he would let us in on his plans. Those six weeks were difficult as we waited to hear from the Lord, but we hung on tightly to our bedrock confidence that when God closes one door, he opens another one.

During those six weeks, while our team was searching for a superior strategy from God, I woke up early one morning.

Instantly God reminded me of Moses leading the children of Israel out of bondage in Egypt. We often think of those scenes in *The Ten Commandments* when the multitude of ex-slaves left through the gates of Egypt on their first steps toward the Promised Land, or the incredible picture of Moses raising his arms when God parted the sea to let the people cross on dry ground. But we don't often think about those first days as Moses confronted Pharaoh. Moses reluctantly answered God's call, but when he ordered Pharaoh to "Let my people go," the Egyptian monarch not only said no; he ordered the slaves to make bricks without straw—and they were furious at Moses! Moses faced many challenges to his leadership, from his people, his opponents, and his own self-doubt, but God strengthened him, and he persevered through the series of plagues inflicted on the hard-hearted Pharaoh and his people. Later, when the Israelites' backs were to the sea and the Egyptian army was threatening them with annihilation, God miraculously intervened again. The Israelites scampered across the sea floor with walls of water on each side, and then they watched as the Egyptian soldiers drowned when they tried to cross.

This is one of the most celebrated moments in the history of our faith, but the wonder and celebration didn't last very long. Only three days later the people struggled in the desert. Instead of trusting God to provide again, they complained. They even told Moses that they had been better off in Egypt as slaves! Can you imagine the discouragement Moses must have felt at that moment?

At Marah, the Israelites found water, but it was bitter to the taste. They grumbled even louder than before. Moses, though, knew where to turn for help. He "cried out to the LORD, and the LORD showed him a piece of wood. He threw it into the water, and the water became sweet" (Exod. 15:25).

The Lord announced that he was testing the people to see if they would trust him. Right after the announcement, God led the people to Elim, a place of twelve springs and seventy palm trees—a place of abundance and hope. But again their contentment didn't last very long. As soon as they reentered the desert, they began to complain about the lack of food and water. God blessed them with manna and quail, but this didn't satisfy their hearts, and they continued to doubt his presence and his provision for them.

Once again as God led them through the desert, the people grew thirsty, but instead of trusting God to provide water and food (as he had many times before), they bitterly griped and quarreled. In fact, the people became so angry that Moses feared they would stone him to death. Moses cried out to the Lord, and God gave him specific directions. He told him to take some of the elders with him and walk ahead of the people, and when they came to the rock at Horeb, to strike it with his staff. Moses did this, and water flowed out.

Again and again God tested the people of Israel to see if they would trust him. These were people who had seen God perform some of the most remarkable miracles in the pages of Scripture: the plagues in Egypt, the pillars of cloud and fire to guide them, the parting of the sea to let them escape the army, water from dry rocks, and manna and quail from the heavens. You would think that these wonders would be enough to convince the people that they could trust God through the next difficulty, but they weren't. God tested the people time after time, and every time they failed the test of faith.

But God didn't just test the people. He also tested the leader he had chosen for them, Moses. Every directive from God, from the burning bush through the events in the wilderness, tested Moses' faith in God's goodness and greatness. When the people grumbled, would Moses grow discouraged as well? When others wanted to go back to Egypt, would he lead the retreat? When his own brother gave up on him and made a golden calf for the people to worship, would he give up on the mission and walk away in disgust? And when God corrected him, would he pout in self-pity or take it in humble submission?

That morning, as I read through these chapters in Exodus, God met with me and spoke to my heart. He reminded me that every transition is full of tests—for our people, for our leaders, and for me. He said to me, "You and your people are wandering in the desert of ambiguity, not knowing which way to turn. I want you to know that all of this isn't an accident. It's a test. Will you trust me? Will you look to me to lead you and provide for you? Will you wait patiently for me to give you the answers you need? You are at the waters of Marah, and the water is bitter. Will you trust me to make it sweet? That's what I want to do, but I won't perform the miracle of leading you by pillars of fire and cloud unless you trust in me. And when you trust me and I lead you, it won't be the end of the testing. Just as I kept testing Moses and the people of Israel time after time, I'll keep testing you to see if you'll trust me. If you do, I'll turn every bitter moment into sweet blessings, and I'll turn every setback into new strategies that propel your ministry forward."

I began to realize that my complaining and worrying had been going on for more than a few weeks. These concerns and doubts had been eating at me for almost a year. I had complained to God time after time for not providing the answers I wanted, in my way and in my time—just like the children of Israel. For the past year God had been testing me, holding back his direction. But now God was saying, "Go to this rock and hit it, and the water will flow. Now is the time."

He reminded me that every transition is full of tests—for our people, for our leaders, and for me.

During the previous year my frustrations were compounded by a sense that because I lacked answers, I wasn't a good leader. Anger and shame aren't the best foundation for having a relationship with God, but in his mercy God is infinitely patient and kind to us. To be a good leader of God's people, I didn't have to have all the answers. All I had to do was remind the people that we were going to trust God together to lead us and that we'd follow him wherever he directed us to go.

When the time was right, the Lord taught me one of the most valuable lessons in leadership: wait for the Lord's answer, in his timing. If we will walk by faith in God's goodness, we can face our doubts with the certainty of God's promises. King David wrote about the certainty we can have as we wait. He assures us,

> I wait for the LORD, my soul waits,
>   and in his word I put my hope.
> My soul waits for the Lord
>   more than watchmen wait for the morning,
>   more than watchmen wait for the morning.
> — PSALM 130:5–6

I love that image. Think about it: How certain are the watchmen on the city walls that the sun will come up the next morning? Pretty certain, I'd say! They exhibit both great certainty and expectation that morning will come. These men have the responsibility to look for enemies who might try to sneak up on the city to attack it. All night they strain their eyes to see in the dark, but they know that the light will reveal the truth. They wait, but not complacently. They peer intently in the first light to see if any enemy soldiers are attacking. They expect the sunlight to give them the answers they need. And like them we wait expectantly, as certain as the next morning's sunrise, knowing that God will reveal himself and his direction for us when the time is right.

A major—actually, *the* major—part of keeping our vision fresh is to deepen our dependence on God, to see every difficulty as a test instituted by God instead of a random roadblock. We respond in a very different way when we realize that the daily struggles of life are all tests to see if we truly trust in the strength and wisdom of the Lord. Instead of complaining, we turn to him for guidance. Instead of getting angry with the people who seem to get in the way, we find ways to encourage them and we ask them to be partners with us. Instead of assuming that we're defective leaders because we don't know what to do, we realize that the greatest leaders of all time (Moses, Joshua, David, and the rest) lived in ambiguity. The difference is that they accepted their situation and trusted God to give them hope and help in his timing.

> A major—actually, *the* major—part of keeping our vision fresh is to deepen our dependence on God.

MANAGE PEOPLE'S EXPECTATIONS

Periods of transition in the life of a church will also bring times of great frustration. It's a given, so you might as well accept it. Imparting a fresh sense of vision and a new strategy raises expectations to new heights, but it also uncovers latent fears. People will be excited about the possibilities ... until they realize that the changes will affect them personally and make them uncomfortable. They may have to change roles, and there will be changes in relationships as well. Whether the change happens gradually or suddenly, they begin to grasp the inescapable fact that life is going to be different in the future. "Actually," they may become convinced, "fulfilling a bigger vision for God isn't that great after all. In fact, I don't like it one bit! And come to think of it, this is just the pastor's idea. Why is he pushing this on me?"

Ever heard that before? I hope not, but I'd imagine that if people were really honest with you about their hopes and fears, you'd hear it a lot more often. Change and growth sound very attractive to most people, as long as they affect someone else.

> Change and growth sound very attractive to most people, as long as they affect someone else.

Although most people will respond in the way we've just discussed, there are always a few intrepid souls who respond in the *opposite* way. They long for the growth and change to happen, and they're frustrated when it doesn't happen soon enough. For the first group, present reality feels comfortable, but for this group, the status quo feels like a limitation. They want more, and they can't wait to get where God is leading them.

It doesn't matter if we're thrilled or terrified as we anticipate the future; the source of our frustration and fear is the same. It's the gap between our expectations and reality. This principle is true in every organization: churches, teams, families, etc. If I tell my wife, Jenni, that I'm going to be home at 6:00 p.m. but I don't get home until 8:00 p.m., she'll look at me when I walk through the door and ask, "Where were you? We waited for dinner, but the children got hungry. Why didn't you call?" Or if I tell my staff and board, "We're going to reach this goal by this date," but the date comes and goes without progress toward the objective, they have every right to ask, "Pastor Scott, what happened? I thought God was leading us, but we didn't hit our target." I may have been working hard behind the scenes, and we may have made tremendous progress, but if they haven't seen the steps, they will wonder about my leadership.

In both scenarios, good communication could have saved the day. If I had called Jenni at 5:45 p.m. to tell her I'd be late, everything would have been fine — no frustration for her, and no guilt for me. And if I had given our staff and board intermediate benchmarks to show we were making progress, they would have celebrated the progress we were making, instead of wondering what had happened. Poor communication leads to heightened frustration and fear because it fails to manage the expectations of others. To keep the vision fresh during times of transition, we need to work hard to communicate clearly and often, not only about the lofty goals but also about every step along the way. Those who are eager to fulfill the vision will see each step as confirmation, and those who are afraid of the future will be reassured by the constant flow of information.

To reduce frustration and fear in times of change, keep the vision fresh by doing the following things:

> *Give regular progress reports.* The accountants on your board and your staff will want to see the spreadsheets, but most people go brain-dead when they encounter that level of detail. In every staff meeting and board meeting, try to paint a verbal picture of your progress toward the ultimate goal. This keeps the vision in front of people, and it lets them get excited about each incremental step along the way.
>
> *Share setbacks as well as successes.* When Japan surrendered to the Allies at the end of World War II, the Japanese civilians were shocked because they had been repeatedly told

that they were winning the war. If you experience setbacks, don't hide them from your staff and key leaders. Be honest, and explain what you're doing to remedy the problem.

Give credit to others, but refuse to point fingers of blame. These reports can be times of genuine celebration about what God has done, and times to affirm those who have worked creatively and tenaciously. Be generous and gracious in your praise, and never point fingers when you've hit a snag. If you've failed, admit it. People will be amazed by your honesty, and they'll trust you even more. When others fail, ask, "How can I help?" They'll appreciate your gracious offer, and they'll probably do far better next time.

Explain how fulfilling the grand vision will affect individuals and families. Some of us get excited about new buildings and big budgets, but that's not what makes most of us tick. We want to hear stories about real people whose lives are being transformed even by the hope of growth in the church. Describe the plight of families you'll be able to touch. Keep the vision personal and gripping.

Remind people that we're trusting God together. Obviously, blessings come from the hand of God, but tests do too. No matter how well or how badly things seem to be going, and no matter how clear or how muddy the vision looks today, focus your heart on the character of God. Thank him for his goodness, praise him for his greatness, and trust him to lead you in the next step. Thank God for those who are leading the charge toward the future, and trust him to use those who are hesitant, to sharpen you and teach you to depend on him even more.

A compelling vision doesn't stay sharp on its own. Entropy, the tendency toward disintegration, operates in every realm, including the world of a growing church. One of the primary tasks for us as leaders is to continually inject life into the system so people remember why we've moved them from comfort into chaos. We've addressed the fact that our families, our staff teams, and our lay leaders will experience fear and frustration in the gap between expectation and present reality, but remember that you'll experience those emotions too. You can't avoid it. They're part of the equation for a visionary leader. But you don't have to face these times alone. A life coach can give you insight and encouragement drawn from years of experience, and you'll not only survive these turbulent times—you'll thrive.

MAPPING YOUR DIRECTION

1. Describe the differences between a vision and a vehicle (or strategy) to get there.

2. Have you seen people in your church misunderstand the difference between an ironclad vision and a flexible strategy? Describe the difficulties this has caused.

3. What are some ways in which recognizing every difficulty as a test helps you stay on track with God and with the vision? What are some tests you've experienced? How did you fare in them?

4. What are some ways in which people express their fears and frustrations when they face the gap between present reality and their expectations?

5. Write a few specific ways in which you can communicate more effectively to manage people's expectations during transitions.

6. How can you manage your own fears and frustrations during these times?

CHAPTER 10

ENDURANCE

Staying the Course

You don't judge a team by its record, but by its heart and
tenacity—two things you either have or you don't have.
— REGGIE SANDERS, MAJOR-LEAGUE BASEBALL PLAYER

In the spring of 1914 Ernest Shackleton was looking for a few
good men. It was the age of polar exploration. In April 1909,
United States Navy engineer Robert Peary claimed to have
reached the North Pole. The close race to reach the South Pole
was won by Roald Amundsen, who arrived on December 14,
1911, only a month before Robert Scott. Still, no one had ever
crossed the continent of Antarctica, and Shackleton was eager to
lead the expedition. He wrote, "After the conquest of the South
Pole by Amundsen who, by a narrow margin of days only, was
in advance of the British Expedition under Scott, there remained
but one great main object of Antarctic journeyings—the crossing
of the South Polar continent from sea to sea."

Shackleton had been on a failed expedition only a few years
before, so he had no illusions about the difficulty the men faced.
He placed an ad in the newspaper to recruit the kind of men
he needed. It read, "Men wanted for hazardous journey. Small
wages, bitter cold, long months of complete darkness, constant
danger, safe return doubtful. Honor and recognition in case of
success."

Five thousand men applied, and they were carefully screened.
By August Shackleton had selected twenty-seven men for his
crew, and the ship *Endurance* was ready to sail. Soon after they

left British waters, however, rumors of impending war with Germany proved true, and Europe erupted in combat. Shackleton cabled the Lord of the Admiralty, Winston Churchill, offering his entire command to the war effort, but Churchill responded with instructions for Shackleton's expedition to continue to the pole and across the continent of Antarctica. Churchill's telegram consisted of a single word: "Proceed."

The *Endurance* reached the British whaling outpost of South Georgia Island in the South Atlantic, and from there it began its voyage to the Weddell Sea and Antarctica. The ship encountered ice packs far north of where they were expected, and soon the ship made only halting progress through the ice. To pass the time, Shackleton and his men played soccer and chipped ice from around the ship, but the weather gradually grew colder, and the ship stuck fast in the ice. They had no choice now but to wait until the next spring.

On a particularly cold night, the heavy timbers of the *Endurance* began to groan from the enormous pressure of the pack ice. Shackleton ordered his men to leave the relative warmth of the ship and set up camp about one hundred yards away. But soon, during another cold night, they heard the crack of timbers. The ice slowly crushed their ship as they watched helplessly. For several months they had been beyond contact with the outside world. They were on their own, drifting on pack ice in the most desolate part of the globe.

Shackleton battled the problem of boredom among the crew by having each man teach the others the particular skills he had brought to the expedition. They played soccer when the weather cleared, and during the warmer months they spent time hunting seals and penguins for fresh meat. The dangers, however, weren't confined to the cold. Massive leopard seals, with razor-sharp teeth, and killer whales prowled those waters. The whales had perfected a hunting technique unique to the ice flow. When they spotted some seals, the killer whales dove, then rose at great speed, smashing through the ice to seize unsuspecting seals in their mouths. The men found a hole twenty-five feet in diameter that had been created by a killer whale. One day the crew's photographer, Frank Hurley, took a dog team over the thin ice, and he heard whales blowing behind him. He needed to find thicker ice immediately! He wrote in his diary: "No need to shout 'mush' and swing the lash. The whip of terror had cracked over their heads and they flew before it. The whales behind ... broke through the thin ice as though it were tissue paper, and, I fancy, were so staggered by the strange sight that met their eyes, that for a moment they hesitated. Had they gone ahead and attacked us in front, our chances of escape would have been slim indeed.... Never in my life have I looked upon more loathsome creatures."

Throughout these difficult months, when life seemed so precarious, Shackleton led the men with indomitable good humor. He was never flustered, never confused, and never bitter. The respect of the crew for their leader grew each day as they watched him cheerfully face each daunting difficulty.

After being on the ice flow for fifteen months, Shackleton and his crew made a dash in three small boats to Elephant Island. They succeeded, but they knew they couldn't last long on that deserted spit of land. Shackleton made the fateful decision to take a few men and try to navigate across the treacherous South Atlantic to South Georgia. Only a few days later they took their bearings and sailed northeast toward a dot in the middle of the ocean, eight hundred miles away.

The crew of six in the tiny boat used their sextant to determine their location and direction, but their sightings were made far more difficult in fierce South Atlantic storms that created one-hundred-foot swells! The storms, however, drove the little boat at an alarming speed, and though the journey had been expected to take a month, Shackleton and the five men saw the cliffs of South Georgia in only two weeks.

Howling winds and stiff currents prevented them from sailing around the island to the whaling center. They beached on the opposite shore and trudged over the glacier and mountains to the little village below — a hike that was thought impossible by even the most skilled and rested climbers. The next morning, they reached the tiny village, and they knocked on the door of the harbormaster. When he opened the door, he didn't even recognize the dirty, disheveled men he had last seen less than two years before.

Shackleton immediately enlisted a ship to go back to Elephant Island to rescue the waiting men. Amazingly, through the entire ordeal, every man survived. They had failed to reach their objective of crossing the continent on foot, but they had a story to tell like none other. The story, though, was not just of incredible daring and unimaginable hardships; it was of a leader who refused to give up or complain. Shackleton's bravery and his skill as a leader of men have become legendary. Seldom has anyone been praised so highly for an expedition that failed its mission, but seldom has anyone led under such hostile conditions with such skill, daring, and unstoppable optimism. The tenacity to endure during difficult times is one of the most important traits of a leader.

CREATED TO LEAD

People who want to avoid problems shouldn't attempt steering through chaos. During times of transition, problems are unavoidable. In fact, we often create them as we push forward and change the existing reality. But true leaders like Ernest Shackleton are willing to forge ahead regardless of obstacles. Leaders don't just lead through smooth waters and pleasant breezes; they lead through the storms and tempests as well.

> People who want to avoid problems shouldn't attempt steering through chaos. During times of transition, problems are unavoidable.

Great leaders show their mettle as they point the way into the unknown. Like Paul, who was both a visionary and a shepherd, they realize that they were born to take people where they'd never go on their own. All of us have been created by God and infused with talents and abilities to accomplish God-sized visions. Paul explained it this way to the Ephesians: "We are God's workmanship, created in Christ Jesus to do good works, which God prepared in advance for us to do" (Eph. 2:10).

As leaders, we're most *fulfilled* when we're inspiring people around us to reach for more than they've ever grasped before. We're most *effective* when we marshal every resource to meet

TIPS FOR TRANSITIONS
Greg Surratt
Seacoast Church: Mount Pleasant, South Carolina

It feels as if the community I give leadership to, Seacoast Church, has been in a constant state of transition since we started over twenty years ago. I sometimes wish we would finally arrive somewhere, but I'm not sure that's really our goal. Transitioning is the state of going from one place to another. The alternative to transitions is going nowhere—staying in the same place. Since the winds of the Holy Spirit are constantly moving and changing, our churches should be constantly reshaping for the journey. Maybe being in constant transition is a good thing after all.

While we have in no way "arrived" when it comes to negotiating change, I'd like to share three simple lessons that we try to apply to new transitional challenges.

1. *Words are really important.* I remember that when we were trying to transition our church into being more "seeker accessible," we made a really big mistake with the language we were using. We saw a bulletin from another church that had a disclaimer that read something like, "If you are a seeker here today, this service is designed for you. If you are a believer, we have a midweek service that goes more in depth into God's Word." I thought that sounded great, so we began to run a similar blurb in our bulletin. Immediately our seasoned church people began to complain that the weekend teaching was becoming progressively more shallow. The truth is, I hadn't changed anything about the way I was preaching. All that had changed was those few lines in the weekly bulletin. Since I'm such an astute student of change, I quickly repositioned the words to say something like, "If you are a seeker OR a seasoned believer, you're going to LOVE our weekend services." Amazingly, over time, people marveled at how much deeper the teaching was getting, when the only thing that had changed was a wiser use of words. You've heard the phrase "Them's fightin' words"? (If you live in the South, you've heard them.) Unfortunately, when used wrongly, words can lead to unnecessary fights

continued on next page...

and quarrels. In a transition, it's important to think very carefully about the words you use.

2. *Always tie the change to the cause.* Some people like change for the sake of change. You might even be one of them. But keep in mind that you are in an *extremely* small minority. Most people will immediately resist change, but if they can see the "why," they can usually follow you to the "where." We try to tie any change we initiate to the shared cause of transformed lives. Whether that's a different style of music, church government, means of outreach, location of ministry, or the name on the sign out front, we tie it to the Jesus mandate to "go and be." If there is not a direct line between the change and the cause, I can predict rough water getting from here to there.

3. *Always try to make friends, not enemies.* Anytime you are trying to steer the ship in a new direction, there will be a certain number of people who are pretty sure you are headed way off course. The more spiritual (religious) they are, the more Scripture they will use, and they will tend to throw in highly charged words and phrases like "Ichabod" (as in "This change assures that the glory has departed from this place"), "compromiser" (as in "If we really loved Jesus, we wouldn't be doing this"), and "the Bible clearly teaches" (as in "If you saw it the way I see it, you'd be closer to right"). When we decided to transition into a multisite church using video teaching, the phrase I seldom heard was "Wow, Greg, that sounds like a great idea." I heard the other words and phrases a lot more often. My natural response is to square my shoulders for a fight and assume an "us versus them" posture. Over the years, I've learned four words that have helped to turn potential enemies into friends of the change. Here they are: *"You might be right."* When a reluctant follower voices concern over the direction we are taking, if we will respond with, "You know, you might be right; tell me why you feel that way," the result is usually a helpful conversation. Often, in the end, you wind up with a passionate evangelist of the proposed change rather than a determined enemy. Granted, this doesn't always happen, but at least you give them a chance to feel that their concerns are being heard. Sometimes it's an opportunity to clean up flawed language and tie your future communication more closely to the cause. And besides, I think I remember Jesus saying something once about the benefits of being a peacemaker. If you're going to lead through multiple transitions, you are going to need all the friends you can get!

needs others have seen but don't know how to meet. And we're most *satisfied* when we are convinced in the depths of our hearts that what we're doing is the work God has given us to do.

RUN ... AND KEEP RUNNING

God never promised that leading his people would be easy. Every great leader in the Scriptures and throughout church history faced internal and external struggles: doubt and opposition, fear and hesitation, weariness and demonic attack. To fulfill our God-given calling, we need more than a great plan and a lot of initial energy—we need the tenacity to endure. The writer to the Hebrews understood this necessity, and he encourages us to run life's race as a marathon instead of a sprint. He writes to first-century Christians who are suffering persecution because of their faith. Under intense pressure, some of them are considering going back to Judaism. He wants them and us to understand that we're not alone, and if we focus properly and refuse to quit, we'll reach the finish line.

He begins, "Since we are surrounded by such a great cloud of witnesses, let us throw off everything that hinders and the sin that so easily entangles, and let us run with perseverance the race marked out for us" (Heb. 12.1). When we're in the midst of chaos, we may feel terribly alone. Our staff members don't understand why we're charting a new course when things are going just fine right now. Board members keep asking the same questions over and over again, and after we drag ourselves in each night, our spouses look at us and wonder, "Are you sure this is what God wants you to do? It's killing you, and I have to put a picture of you on the table at dinner so the children will remember what you look like!" But we aren't alone. In the previous chapter, the writer of Hebrews has just given us several thumbnail sketches of men and women who trusted God through dark times. These are the heroes of the faith. Their stories inspire us, but they do something more. The writer tells us that these saints of the past are watching us run our race, and they're leading the cheers in heaven! Daniel is yelling, "Keep praying no matter what. Don't let the people of this world intimidate you. God will protect you, and he will promote you when the time is right." David cheers, "Don't let the giants in your life push you around. Recognize that God is waiting for someone who will have the courage to believe in him and run to the battle to defeat the giants." Jonah seems a bit chastened as he yells, "Don't run from God. Run with him. His way is better. Believe me. I know." And Moses' voice booms, "When you feel you're in an impossible situation and there's no hope, trust God to make a way. Even if your back is to an ocean and an army is about to attack, trust him. Believe me. He'll make a way where there is no way."

Let's look at some principles from this passage that will help us endure.

Lighten Your Load

As we run the marathon of leadership, the writer of Hebrews tells us to "throw off everything that hinders and the sin that so easily entangles." The Greek word for "hinders" is the same word used to describe the excess weight runners needed to lose in order for them to run at their best. When we watch college and Olympic track athletes, we see that they minimize the weight of every article of clothing. They wear the flimsiest shorts, thin tank tops, and feather-light shoes. No pockets full of stuff. No long pants or sweaters. No backpacks. Nothing that would slow them down. The writer of Hebrews isn't just talking about sin. Certainly, sin slows us down, but he wants us to be more ruthless than that. He encourages us to throw off the habits that distract us, the desires that absorb our time, steal our energy, and rob us of passion. These may be different for each of us, but our culture has no lack of these things. For some it might be watching too many movies, for others, too much ESPN. Maybe you spend too much time reading novels or eating or surfing the internet or reading blogs or taking too much caffeine or any of the multitude of things that can get in the way of you being your best for God.

Distractions weigh us down, but sin is like a rope tied around our ankles. We simply can't run the race if our legs are entangled by sin. As we all know, sins come in all shapes and sizes, from the covert to the obvious, the ones we desperately try to hide and those we shamelessly boast about. What sins do you wrestle with? Which ones consistently trip you up? We may have a secret addiction, or our hearts and minds may be consumed with envy that someone else is getting more applause. We don't need to go into lists here. The Holy Spirit convicts believers of sin, and if you'll stop and ask, you can be sure he'll show you anything in your life that displeases him.

Let's be honest. Sin is very attractive. From the first temptation in the Garden to the ones we face today, the temptation of sin is that a behavior, attitude, or relationship will give us what we really want—apart from God. We may know that it's wrong, but we still have a perverse desire to find out just how close we can get to the flame without being burned. Then, when we inevitably fall, we feel intense shame and guilt, but we believe we can't tell anybody about our moral failure, or we'll lose credibility. Hiding our secrets from others wears us out and distracts us from God's purposes. Gradually (or not so gradually) we begin to live a lie, telling others and ourselves that we're "doing just fine" as we hide the shameful reality of our secret.

For God's sake, for your sake, for your family's sake, and for the sake of God's eternal purposes for the people you lead, "man up"—throw off the distractions and the sins in your life. Be honest and confess your failure. Lighten your load so you can run the race God has for you.

Run *Your* Race

Comparison will eat your lunch. I know because it's happened to me. I've looked around at other pastors and thought, "Man, I wish God would use me like that!" or, "Hey, I'm doing better than that guy." Comparing our abilities and effectiveness with those of others may seem very natural (because everybody does it), but it's deadly. The writer to the Hebrews tells us to run our own race in the lane where God has placed us. We can certainly learn wonderful things from others, but we need to be careful not to slip over the line to envy or mimicking, wanting what someone else has or copying another's model without praying and reflecting.

Earlier I shared a story about a stressful time in my life when God woke me up and put a word on my tongue: *focus*. That morning I realized I was far too busy doing things I didn't need to be doing. I had equated busyness with devotion, but that was a deceptive lie. I was too enamored with pleasing others instead of first and foremost pleasing the Lord.

If I say yes too often, I dilute my effectiveness and rob others of the joy of meeting that need.

I wish I could say that I learned my lesson that morning and I've never struggled with it since, but that would be a lie. I struggle with busyness and working hard to please other people all the time. As a card-carrying member of the fallen human race, I'm tempted to measure my value against others if I'm not careful. If I'm doing better than them, I feel good. If they're surpassing me, I feel lousy.

One of the hardest—and most necessary—lessons I'm learning is the importance of staying focused by saying no to anything God hasn't assigned me to do. I don't want to disappoint people, so when they ask me if I can help them, I have a hard time saying no. If I say yes too often, I dilute my effectiveness and rob others of the joy of meeting that need. I'm actually stealing passion and joy from two people: myself and another servant God wants to use.

Keep Your Head Up

The writer of Hebrews encourages us, "Let us fix our eyes on Jesus, the author and perfecter of our faith, who for the joy set before him endured the cross, scorning its shame, and sat down at the right hand of the throne of God" (Heb. 12:2). I run to stay in shape. I can't tell you how often my running partner looks over at me and says, "Scott, keep your head up."

Early in my not-so-illustrious running career, a trainer explained that the posture of our heads determines the airflow to our lungs. If we focus on the ground in front of us (or our shoes as we take the next step, if we're really tired), we constrict the air passage, making it difficult to get the oxygen we need. He recommended, "Run like a string is tied to the top of your head and someone is pulling that string up, causing you to run tall and focused down the track."

This is a perfect metaphor for life as a leader. When we get tired of living and leading, we tend to take our eyes off of the Lord and become fixated on the problems that are right in front of us. When our heads stay down, focused on our problems, we lose perspective. And when our heads are down, the oxygen of faith in Christ becomes constricted, and we get even more exhausted. Sooner or later we feel like quitting.

In one of the most challenging leadership roles in all of history, Nehemiah faced every kind of difficulty as he led the Israelites in rebuilding the wall around Jerusalem. Still, he kept his head up, focused on the Lord's goodness and greatness. The source of strength and passion, he reminded the builders, came from this perspective: "The joy of the LORD is your strength" (Neh. 8:10).

Press On

The writer of Hebrews continues, "Consider [Christ] who endured such opposition from sinful men, so that you will not grow weary and lose heart" (Heb. 12:3). Some of us feel like quitting when people are slow to get on board with our plans, and we get discouraged when people ask too many questions. When we come close to losing heart, we need to think long and hard about Christ's sacrifice for us. Multitudes followed him because he fed them, but when he asked them for a genuine commitment, they melted away. The religious leaders should have welcomed him because they had read about the Messiah in the Scriptures, but they saw him as a threat and plotted his assassination. The night before his execution, he anticipated the pain he would suffer.

He pleaded with the Father for another way, but in the end he accepted the Father's will. His enemies, it seemed, were going to have their way. His closest friends were with him for three years, but at his time of peril they ran away. If it had been me, I would have lost heart about two years earlier! But Jesus endured it all—for you and me. When times are tough, we need to follow his example of faithful tenacity.

Jesus was able to endure the cross because of "the joy set before him." What was the joy that motivated him and led him to the cross? It was twofold. First, Jesus died on the cross because he knew it was the will of his Father, and he delighted in *pleasing him*. Second, he found joy in you and me. He was motivated to go to the cross because he knew that the cross was the only way our sins could be paid for, allowing us to experience his forgiveness, healing, and purpose. His joy was that we could know him here on earth and that we would be with him in heaven forever. Jesus pressed on through the pain and agony of the cross because he wanted to please the Father and save our souls from hell.

> There's a finish line in this race. We aren't going to run forever. And on that day, God will give us an incredible reward for our endurance in following him.

Jesus is the example we should look to when we're weary and feel like quitting. We should call for our friends to stand with us in prayer, and we should call out to the Lord and be honest with him about our fears and our pain. We should give ourselves fully to him and to his will for our lives, and he'll give us the strength to keep going. How do we press on? In the same way Jesus kept going. We endure our troubles because our joy is to please the Father and because we know that one day we are going to be with Jesus in heaven. There's a finish line in this race. We aren't going to run forever. And on that day, God will give us an incredible reward for our endurance in following him.

Be at Peace with the Pace

We believe in miracles, but sometimes the miracle God gives is the strength to endure rather than an instantaneous solution to our problem. God's purposes are far beyond our understanding, and his perspective goes beyond our limited vision. His goal isn't just to bless the next great program for our church. He wants to touch lives, and he graciously works through our programs, but in the process his larger goal is the shaping of our character. Like a wise, attentive dad, God directs our lives and disciplines us. The writer of Hebrews says, "Endure hardship as discipline; God is treating you as sons. For what son is not disciplined by his father?... No discipline seems pleasant at the time, but painful. Later on, however, it produces a harvest of righteousness and peace for those who have been trained by it" (Heb. 12:7, 11).

Difficulties are a normal part of being a child of God. They aren't signs of God's punishment, and they aren't indicators that God is taking a nap or doesn't care about our lives. Good fathers teach their children important lessons, often through tests and struggles, to sharpen them for the future.

When I was twelve years old, my mother and father were leading a trip to the Holy Land to visit the places we had read about in the Bible. I wanted to go with them, but I didn't have the money to pay for the trip. My dad could have paid for my travel expenses, or he could have asked some friends for the money, but he had a different agenda for me. He told me I could go *if* I would raise the money. For six or seven months before the trip, he arranged different jobs for me. He took me out to the woods to cut down trees, and I cut the logs into firewood. I set up shop on the side of the road to sell it. He talked to a farmer who went to our church, and the farmer allowed me to harvest a field of his watermelons. Again I sold them on the side of the road. Dad connected me with a builder who was developing some property. I gathered the trash and cleaned the lots. It was hard work, but I was able to make enough money to cover about half the cost of the trip.

Every night, Dad and I prayed that God would provide the money for me to go, and every night, my dad encouraged me to trust God for his provision. A couple of weeks before we were to go, I was still hundreds of dollars short. Still, Dad encouraged me to trust God to provide. I didn't know it, but a man in the church had approached my dad several weeks earlier and told him that he would give any amount I was lacking. My dad thanked him, but he also said, "Let's not tell Scott." The man asked why, and my dad explained, "I don't want to interrupt what God is doing in Scott's life. God is growing him up through this process, and we don't want to hinder it in any way."

I'll never forget that trip, but even more, I'll always remember my dad teaching me the value of work and faith in God. Dad didn't want to just give me a ten-day, life-changing experience in Israel. He wanted to give me a six-month, life-building process that would develop character and discipline in my life. Why? Because he loved me, and in his wisdom, he knew it would make me a better man.

God has the same purpose in the difficulties we face each day. Often, when we don't understand his purposes, we try to find relief as quickly as possible. But relief from our struggles may not be the best classroom for the lessons God wants us to learn. We can pray for a miracle, but we need to accept God's answer of yes, no, or wait as his decree. Quite often he says, "Yes, but it will be a process," and over time we learn to trust God more than ever before. The pace may be slower than we'd like, but we're wise to accept God's timetable and be at peace with the pace.

> Relief from our struggles may not be the best classroom for the lessons God wants us to learn.

I've been running lately to lose some weight and be a good steward of the Lord's temple. My youngest son, Dakota, has been running with me in the evenings. The first couple of times we ran together, I tried to tell him that a steady pace enables runners to go a long way. Did he listen to me? Of course not. He was excited, and he started running ahead of me. I yelled, "Son, slow down. Come run with me."

But he yelled back, "Dad, you're too slow!" I don't think he meant for me to hear his next words, but sound traveled well that night. He said, "And you're boring."

I laughed. "That may be true, but you need to stay with me." I tried to explain. "Son, we're on a busy road, and I want you close to me for safety reasons. And we're going a couple of miles. If we run too fast at the start, we won't be able to finish."

He didn't like it, but he slowed down and ran by my side. About three-quarters of a mile into the run, Dakota looked really tired. He asked if we could walk a while or take a break.

As leaders, we hear God's voice, and we get a clear vision of what he wants to do through us. We get so excited that we want to run fast from the start. When God doesn't seem to move as fast as we want to go, we get frustrated. We want him to move faster, and we get bored because the process is taking so long. We don't realize that we aren't yet ready to run faster. So our loving heavenly Father says, "Son, stay with me. I want you by my side to protect you, and I want to help you build up to the next level. But for now, be faithful at this pace."

When we stop to think about it, we quickly remember that God is the author and perfecter of life, the Alpha and the Omega, the source of wisdom, forgiveness, and power. We can trust him! He loves every person on the planet with a fierce, unstoppable passion. We can trust his judgment. His plans are good and right, and his timing is impeccable. We can trust his pace of progress. He knows what he's doing. I may get frustrated over how long it's taking us to build the new sanctuary, raise the money at our church, or provide the staff and places to expand our multisite ministry. I want it to be done *now* and paid for *yesterday*. But God is at work—not only on the project but also in the process. And God is at work on me as the pastor. He is getting us ready so we not only move into a bigger space but also move in as bigger people.

God is at work—not only on the project but also in the process.

God could fulfill all of our needs for buildings, staff, money, volunteers, and everything else in a sudden, miraculous way (and I'd take it if that happened!), but I believe he wants us to grow in faithfulness, hope, and patience as we trust him in the process. As we run, he wants us to develop our prayer muscles, our giving muscles, and our faith muscles, but this won't happen unless we are put in a position where we have to use them.

AS YOU GO

Whether you are a pastor or a staff member or serve on the board of a local church, you have been chosen by almighty God to serve him. It is an unspeakable privilege, a high honor, and a solemn responsibility. In these pages, we've examined a number of principles that can help you and your church move through transitions with wisdom and strength. But these principles aren't divorced from spiritual power. In each chapter, we've stressed the necessity of putting Christ in the center of every desire, every plan, and every step. Above all, as you think about moving into and through transitions in your church, listen to him and answer his call.

MAPPING YOUR DIRECTION

1. Does the story of Ernest Shackleton inspire you or overwhelm you? Explain your answer. Do you see any similarities between his story and yours?

2. What are some weights that hinder your running? What are some sins that entangle you? What are some ways in which you will lighten your load?

3. What are some ways in which comparison gets us off track? How can you recognize it when you're comparing yourself with others? What will you do about it?

4. What are some of the negative things that happen when we focus on the problems right in front of us instead of keeping our heads up and riveting our attention on Christ?

5. In the past, what are some things that have caused you to "grow weary and lose heart" (Heb. 12:3)? How does considering Christ give us insight, tenacity, and strength?

6. In what kinds of situations do you tend to be impatient? What can you do to be more at peace with God's pace?

7. Now that you've finished this book, how do you plan to implement the principles you've learned?

8. What's your next step?

NOTES

1. John McGahern, *All Will Be Well: A Memoir* (New York: Knopf, 2005), 189.

2. Nicholar Carr, *The Big Switch: Rewiring the World, from Edison to Google* (New York: Norton, 2008), 228.

3. David Abulafia, *The Discovery of Mankind: Atlantic Encounters in the Age of Columbus* (New Haven: Yale Univ. Press, 2008).

4. *Inspirational and Devotional Verse* (Grand Rapids, Mich.: Zondervan, 1946), 266.

5. Holmes and Rahe, "The Survey of Recent Events," cited in Kaplan and Saccuzzo, *Psychological Testing: Principles, Applications, and Issues* (Pacific Grove, Calif.: Brooks/Cole, 1989), 445–47.

6. J. I. Packer, *Knowing God* (Downers Grove, Ill.: InterVarsity, 1973), 91–93. Note: I changed his metaphor of a train signal station to that of air traffic controllers.

7. In this book, I use *board* to mean the lay leadership team for our church. Other church polity may use *deacons*, *elders*, or some other language to describe this group of leaders. We changed the name of this group from deacon board to board of elders because the term *elder* emphasizes the need for them to hear from God as we lead the church.

8. Malcolm Gladwell, *The Tipping Point: How Little Things Can Make a Big Difference* (New York: Back Bay Books, 2002), 7–13.

9. Jim Collins, *Good to Great* (New York: HarperBusiness, 2001), 165–66.

10. John Ortberg, "Diagnosing Hurry Sickness," *Leadership* (Fall 1998), www.christianitytoday.com/le/1998/fall/8l4031.html.

11. For more information, go to www.debonoforbusiness.com.

12. For more information, go to www.isixsigma.com.

13. Luci Shaw with Dallas Willard, "Spiritual Disciplines in a Postmodern World," *Radix* 27, no. 2 (spring 2000): 4–7, 26–31. Online at www.dwillard.org/articles/artview.asp?artid=56.

14. See jan.ucc.nau.edu/~jsa3/hum355/readings/ellul.htm.

15. Max Lucado, *Just Like Jesus* (Nashville: Word, 1998), 27–28.

16. Jim Collins, *Good to Great*, 95–96.

17. Richard Swenson, *Margin: Restoring Emotional, Physical, Financial and Time Reserves to Our Overloaded Lives* (Colorado Springs: NavPress, 2004), 43–52.

Scott Wilson has been in full-time pastoral ministry for more than twenty years. He is the senior pastor of the Oaks Fellowship, located in Dallas, Texas. In the last three years, the church has experienced robust growth, nearly tripling in size—now ministering to nearly three thousand people. The church offers six worship experiences every weekend to accommodate the growing crowds.

Scott is the CEO and founder of Scott Wilson Consulting, an organization that exists to come alongside church and marketplace leaders to enable them to achieve the full potential of what God has called them to do. Pastor Scott has a vision to strengthen and empower God's leaders so they can fulfill their destiny and dreams.

Scott and his father, Dr. Tom Wilson, lead one of the most innovative public school systems in the state of Texas. Life School currently educates over three thousand students in four locations in the Dallas area. Each year, parents camp out overnight to enroll their children in these schools.

Under Scott's visionary leadership, the Oaks School of Leadership was founded in 1998. This school of ministry is in partnership with the Southwestern Assembly of God University in Waxahachie, Texas, and all students receive up to forty-eight university credit hours over a two-year period. They are eligible for grants and loans, as in any other major university. The primary purpose for the Oaks School of Leadership is to train and equip the best leaders in the kingdom of God and to be a leadership pipeline for the multisite ministry of the Oaks and its partners around the world.

Finally, Scott is a loving husband and proud father. Scott and his wife, Jenni, have three boys: Dillon, Hunter, and Dakota. The Wilsons live in the Dallas area.

For more information concerning the Oaks Fellowship and their ministry resources, Scott Wilson Consulting, Life School, the Oaks School of Leadership, or to find a life coach, go to scottwisonleadership.org.

Share Your Thoughts

With the Author: Your comments will be forwarded to
the author when you send them to *zauthor@zondervan.com*.

With Zondervan: Submit your review of this book
by writing to *zreview@zondervan.com*.

Free Online Resources at
www.zondervan.com

Zondervan AuthorTracker: Be notified whenever your favorite
authors publish new books, go on tour, or post an update
about what's happening in their lives at www.zondervan.com/
authortracker.

Daily Bible Verses and Devotions: Enrich your life with daily
Bible verses or devotions that help you start every morning
focused on God. Visit www.zondervan.com/newsletters.

Free Email Publications: Sign up for newsletters on Christian
living, academic resources, church ministry, fiction, children's
resources, and more. Visit www.zondervan.com/newsletters.

Zondervan Bible Search: Find and compare Bible passages in
a variety of translations at www.zondervanbiblesearch.com.

Other Benefits: Register yourself to receive online benefits
like coupons and special offers, or to participate in research.

ZONDERVAN.com/
AUTHORTRACKER
follow your favorite authors